# leadership

# leadership

**2nd edition**

**philip sadler**

mba **masterclass**

**KOGAN PAGE**

London and Sterling, VA

First published in Great Britain and the United States in 2003 by
Kogan Page Limited

120 Pentonville Road
London N1 9JN
UK
www.kogan-page.co.uk

22883 Quicksilver Drive
Sterling VA 20166-2012
USA

ISBN 0 7494 3919 X

---

**British Library Cataloguing-in-Publication Data**

A CIP record for this book is available from the British Library.

---

**Library of Congress Cataloging-in-Publication Data**
Sadler, Philip, 1930–
    Leadership / Philip Sadler.
        p. cm. – (MBA masterclass series)
Includes bibliographical references and index.
    ISBN 074943919X
    1. Leadership. I. Title. II. Series.
    HD57.7.S227 2003
    658.4′092–dc21

                                                                    2002154865

---

Typeset by JS Typesetting Ltd, Wellingborough, Northants
Printed and bound in Great Britain by Biddles Ltd, Guildford and King's Lynn
*www.biddles.co.uk*

# Contents

# The series editor

Philip Sadler is a Vice President of the Ashridge Business School where he was chief executive for 20 years. He now divides his time between writing, speaking, consultancy and voluntary service. He is a Fellow of the International Academy of Management, a Board Member of the International Leadership Association, a Companion of the Institute of Management, a Fellow of the Institute for Personnel and Development, a Fellow of the Institute of Directors, and a Patron of the Centre for Tomorrow's Company.

He has been awarded the honorary degrees of DSc (City University) and DBA (De Montford University). He holds the Burnham Gold Medal of the Institute of Management and was appointed CBE in 1986.

His recent books include *Managing Change* (1995), *Leadership* (2003), *The Seamless Organization* (2001) and *Building Tomorrow's Company* (2002).

# Introduction

## WHY LEADERSHIP?

Until relatively recently the word leadership did not feature very much in management literature. Even as late as 1988 the best selling Gower *Handbook of Management* (Lock, 1988) devoted only two pages to the topic in a volume of over 1200 pages, while the third edition (1992) takes a giant stride, doubling the coverage to four pages! During the 1970s and for much of the early 1980s and '90s developing people for top jobs was seen to be a process of management or executive development, and the process of interaction with face-to-face groups of workers at shop-floor level was referred to as supervision or foremanship.

The emphasis was on the exercise of delegated authority within an orderly framework of job descriptions, reporting relationships and formal procedures to be followed. Leadership was seen as something that the armed forces or politicians engaged in.

Today it is quite different. Leadership is on the agenda in a big way. Books on the subject are streaming on to the market, top industrialists are hailed as great leaders alongside the great military and political leaders of the age and leadership 'gurus' have emerged from academic obscurity.

Why has this happened? Not, in my view, because of any really significant breakthroughs in our understanding of the process as a result of academic research in this field, although in the US particularly there has been a great deal of research into the subject, much of it funded by the armed services. The main reasons appear to be the following:

▌ The increase in the rate of change in the business environment. When the situation is relatively stable the need to arouse enthusiasm, to energize people, to persuade them to give up cherished ideas and working practices is less than when there is a strong requirement for change, particularly radical change. Management, it seems, is perfectly adequate when things are routine and predictable, but when the organisation hits turbulence and uncertainty leadership is called for. This idea has been confirmed in our minds as we have observed dramatic transformations in British industry in recent times which appear to be due more to inspirational leadership than to good management as traditionally conceived. British Airways under Colin Marshall, and ICI under John Harvey-Jones are oft-quoted examples.

▌ Second, case studies of firms which were very successful in a sustained way over many years, such as the study of lasting success in US industry *Built to Last* (Collins and Porras, 1994), have produced convincing evidence to show that success has been associated with effective leadership from the top exercised by deeply respected founders or chief executives such as Bill Hewlett of Hewlett Packard, Colonel Johnson of Johnson & Johnson or George Merck of Merck.

▌ Third, a new generation of 'gurus' led by Tom Peters, articulate and persuasive, have produced massive anecdotal evidence, mainly from US industry, but including such European business leaders as Percy Barnevik of ABB and Jan Carlzon of SAS, to convince us that leadership really does make a difference.

As a result leadership is increasingly a subject in the syllabi of MBA programmes and leadership training and development programmes of various kinds are offered by many business schools. The assumption behind these programmes is that leadership can be taught; or at least that it is something that is capable of being developed. There is increasing acceptance that this is so, but relatively little agreement about *how* it can be developed successfully.

## THE SOURCES OF IDEAS ABOUT LEADERSHIP

The ideas and theories of leadership drawn upon in this book are derived from several sources:

I **Academic research.** These range from laboratory experiments involving subjects (usually university students) often with little or no experience of, or involvement in, organizational life, to surveys of the attitudes and behaviours of real business leaders or of the people subject to their leadership, which are then linked to some measures of organisational effectiveness. The results of these studies are usually published in academic journals and rarely come to the attention of actual business leaders unless they are studying for a Master's degree. The articles often use pretentious or 'esoteric' language which, while they may add to the academic reputation and respectability of the authors, tend to alienate practising managers. A good example is an article published in the journal *Group and Organisation Management* (June 1996), with the title, 'A syncretical model of charismatic/transformational leadership'. According to *Chambers Dictionary*, a syncretical model would be one which attempted to effect a reconciliation or compromise between different sets of beliefs. To use a well-known phrase, 'Not many people know that', including the compilers of the Microsoft spell check. This article is, in fact, both useful and relevant; the point being made, however, is that few managers would be bothered to read it and find out.

I **Popularizing academics.** These are people who from a position of professorial eminence in an academic institution of high repute write fluently and with authority on leadership but whose views are not necessarily the outcome of rigorous academic research. Indeed they are sometimes based largely on anecdotal evidence, or on interviews with small samples of business leaders. They should have a knowledge of the more rigorous research carried out elsewhere, although this is not always evident. Their statements and opinions carry the ring of conviction and certainty. Several of them are themselves quite charismatic when speaking in public. They often have a strong following among practising managers, their books are widely read and they command large fees for their public appearances. They are seldom able, however, to draw on their own experiences, since few have ever held any significant leadership role either in business or academe.

A particular example of the popularizing school is the psycho-analytical approach which sees leadership and followership as a playing out of early life experiences and in particular of the relationships between individuals and their parents.

■ **Consultants.** The consultants who write about leadership have often got closer to the action than the academics but they tend to be less well-grounded in the research and less conceptual in approach. Their writings often appear naïve in comparison and they are particularly prone to come up with yet another list of the personal qualities of the ideal leader.

■ **Practitioners.** The 'I did it my way' group, consisting of real-life leaders (current or retired) giving an account of their approach to leadership. The usefulness of this source for our understanding of the nature of leadership is limited by the natural tendency for people, when writing about themselves, to be selective and lacking in objectivity.

■ **Biographical studies.** These can be expected to be more objective and hence more illuminating than leaders' own accounts of their experience, providing they are not tinged with hero worship.

■ **Summarizers.** Those who attempt to draw together material from all the above sources and draw out the major lessons to be learned. (This book represents one such attempt.)

The literature on leadership is more extensive than impressive. It contains more in the way of myth and legend than fact or substance. Much of it is highly subjective and approaches the subject within an unacknowledged cultural framework of values and assumptions. It contains a great deal of common sense dressed up as theory, as well as theories which defy common sense. In trying to distil from it all that has been learned, I have tried consistently to bridge the gap between the need on the one hand to have intellectual rigour and a sound conceptual framework and the need on the other not to lose touch with the reality of organizational life.

As the inclusion of this book in the *MBA Masterclass* series indicates, it is designed primarily to meet the needs of students of management on courses leading to an MBA degree or similar qualification. It is equally suitable, however, to all who practise leadership and who would like to gain a better understanding of the process and even, perhaps, draw some inspiration from the ideas it contains.

# 1

# The nature of leadership

## DEFINING LEADERSHIP

There are many, many definitions of leadership. Here are just a few.

An activity or set of activities, observable to others that occurs in a group, organization or institution involving a leader and followers who willingly subscribe to common purposes and work together to achieve them. (Professor Kenneth Clark)

The process of persuasion or example by which an individual (or a leadership team) induces a group to pursue objectives held by the leader or shared by the leader and his or her followers. (John Gardner)

The reciprocal process of mobilizing, by persons with certain motives and values, various economic, political and other resources, in a context of competition and conflict, in order to realize goals independently or mutually held by both leaders and followers. (James McGregor Burns)

Leadership involves influencing task objectives and strategies, influencing commitment and compliance in task behaviour to achieve these objectives, influencing group maintenance and identification and influencing the culture of an organization. (Gary Yuke)

An activity – an influence process – in which an individual gains that trust and commitment of others and without reliance on formal position or authority moves the group to the accomplishment of one or more tasks. (Walter F Ulmer, Jr)

Leadership is the ability to get men to do what they don't like to do and like it. (Harry S Truman)

Leadership, however, is a powerful concept, capable of conveying much more than can be contained within a concise definition and capable of meaning many different things to different audiences in different contexts.

## Process or personal attribute?

Bavelas (1969) draws a distinction between leadership as a *process* (the meaning conveyed in the above definitions) and leadership as a *personal quality*. But there are other meanings; leadership is also a *role* in groups and organizations and when used as *a collective noun* can refer to those responsible for the destiny of a country or a company.

If we look closer at leadership as a process, we can break the concept down into its several parts.

▌ First, the processes involved are such things as influence, exemplary behaviour and persuasion.

▌ Secondly, it involves interaction between actors who are both leaders and followers.

▌ Thirdly, the nature of the interaction is affected by the situation in which it takes place. For example, the interaction between a commander and troops on the battlefield is different in important respects from the interaction between a team leader and a group of scientists in a laboratory.

▌ Finally, the process has various outcomes – most obviously the achievement of goals, but also intermediate outcomes such as the commitment of individuals to such goals, the enhancement of group cohesion and the reinforcement or change of organizational culture.

From this it follows that the study of leadership cannot be validly carried on from a purely psychological perspective. It must be set within the context of the study of the decision-making processes and functioning of organizations.

## Commonalities among leaders

According to Bennis and Nanus (1985), all leaders share three things in common:

1.  All leaders face the challenge of overcoming resistance to change. Some try to do this by the simple exercise of power and control, but effective leaders learn that there are better ways to overcome resistance to change. This involves the achievement of a voluntary commitment to shared values.

2.  A leader often must broker the needs of constituencies both within and outside the organization. The brokering function requires sensitivity to the needs of many stakeholders and a clear sense of the organization's position.

3.  The leader is responsible for the set of ethics or norms that govern the behaviour of people in the organization. Leaders can establish a set of ethics in several ways. One is to demonstrate by their own behaviour their commitment to the set of ethics that they are trying to institutionalise.

According to Bennis (1999), research points to seven attributes essential to leadership:

■ *technical competence:* business literacy and grasp of one's field;

■ *conceptual skill:* a facility for abstract or strategic thinking;

■ *track record:* a history of achieving results;

■ *people skills:* an ability to communicate, motivate, and delegate;

■ *taste:* an ability to identify and cultivate talent;

■ *judgement:* making difficult decisions in a short time frame with imperfect data;

■ *character:* the qualities that define who we are.

One of the problems that occurs frequently in the literature on the subject is the natural and understandable, but potentially misleading, focus on truly great leaders – people of the stature of Gandhi, J F Kennedy, Winston Churchill, Martin Luther King, Nelson Mandela, or Charles de Gaulle. In much the same way, the literature on art or music concentrates on the truly great – Rubens, Renoir, Beethoven and Mozart. Yet in the arts there are thousands upon thousands of talented and accomplished artists and musicians whose creativity, virtuosity and dedication bring pleasure to millions while falling short of being classed as world class. In the same way there are thousands upon thousands of dedicated, effective leaders in organizations and communities of all kinds who inspire others, sustain them through difficult times, lead them into new, uncharted territories, but will never feature in a Tom Peters' video or, indeed, in any list of the world's great leaders. Yet, from a practical point of view, particularly when we are considering how to develop future leaders, we stand to learn more from studying these thousands of working leaders than from focusing on the qualities or behaviour of such as Lee Iacocca or Jack Welch.

## The myths of leadership

Bennis and Nanus (1985) have also identified, through their extensive research, five commonly believed myths surrounding leadership.

1. Leadership is a rare skill. Untrue. While great leaders may be rare, everyone has leadership potential. More important, people may be leaders in one organization and have quite ordinary roles in another. Leadership opportunities are plentiful and within reach of most people.

2. Leaders are born, not made. Not so. The truth is that major capacities and competencies of leadership can be learned, and we are all capable of learning given the will to learn.

3. Leaders are charismatic. Some are, but most are not.

4. Leadership exists only at the top of the organization. In fact, the larger the organization, the more leadership roles it is likely to have.

5. The leader controls and directs. Again, not so. Leadership is not so much the exercise of power as the empowerment of others. Leaders lead by inspiring rather than ordering – by enabling people to use their own initiative and experiences.

Once these myths are cleared away, the question becomes not one of how to become a leader, but rather how to improve one's effectiveness at leadership.

# LEADERSHIP AT DIFFERENT LEVELS

Many of the empirical studies of leadership in industry which involve detailed observation of leaders at work have been focused on the role of the first-line supervisor or middle level manager rather than on chief executives. The reasons for this are several. First, there are more supervisors and managers than CEOs thus providing sizeable samples of leaders. Second, research workers are more likely to be granted facilities to study the behaviour of the supervisor than they are to observe and analyse the activities of top managers. Third, it is perhaps at the level of first-line supervision that the nature of the leadership role is most clear-cut, since the situation involves a group of people with a specific task to perform being led in an immediate and personal way by one appointed to a position of authority over them.

Selznick (1957) has drawn attention to important differences between leadership at lower levels, which he refers to as *interpersonal* leadership, and the kind which takes place in the high echelons of large organizations, which he terms *institutional* leadership. Whereas the task of the former is primarily to achieve routine tasks and to facilitate personal involvement and group working, the role of the latter lies mainly in the field of developing and maintaining systems of beliefs and values. The institutional leader deals with issues in terms of their long-range implications for the organization. His or her major functions are to define policy, to build the kind of social structure which will put that policy into effect, and to maintain the values which will ensure its continuity. At this level of functioning the true contribution of the leader may be made in the course of two or three critical decisions in a year.

Among the studies of leadership at this level one that stands out is the report by Guest (1962) of the leadership behaviour of the chief executive in an automobile assembly plant. At the time this plant was first studied its level of performance, compared with five other similar plants in the same company, was very poor. A year later, a new general manager was assigned to the plant. Within a relatively short time its performance improved dramatically and there were indications of a considerable increase in the favourability of attitudes of employees at all levels. Three years after this a second study of the plant was made in order to trace the reasons for these improvements. It was found that there were few differences in basic organization, comparing the plant under its new leadership with the structure under the previous general manager. It was the view of the researchers that the main reason for the improved performance and morale was the effectiveness of the leadership style of the new chief executive. The findings were in line with Selznick's observations on the functions of high-level leadership in that one notable characteristic of the new manager's approach to his role was his concern with matters relating to future planning. This was in marked contrast to his less successful predecessor, who appeared to act chiefly in response to immediate emergencies.

Dixon (1976) points out that in the military context the qualities required in the exercise of command at one level may not match the qualities required at higher levels. He quotes the Australian Sir John Monash as a brilliant general who was possibly 'an indifferent brigadier, mediocre battalion commander and third rate platoon commander' and suggests that, correspondingly, there have been outstanding platoon and company commanders who, when promoted by reason of their outstanding performance at these lower levels, ended up as incompetent generals. Dixon's example here is Sir Redvers Buller: 'a superb major, a mediocre colonel and an abysmal general'.

Senge (1996) points out that while many executives acknowledge the need for leaders at every level of the organization, they often fail to make the best use of their abilities. They fall into a trap of confusing rank with leadership. The belief that the *leaders* are only those with executive titles and big offices can lead to the lack of initiative, enterprise, and innovation that these same executives rightly say is holding the organization back.

Truly innovative companies, Senge argues, recognize that a dynamic organization needs three kinds of leaders: *local line leaders* (branch managers, project team leaders, sales managers, and other credible front-line performers); *internal networkers* (front-line workers, in-house consultants, trainers, or professional staff who spread ideas throughout the organization); and *executive or top-level leaders*. All three have an essential role to play. Without the initiative and commitment of local line leaders, no change effort will get very far. Without the influence of internal networkers, innovative practices rarely spread across the organization. Without the vision of executive leadership, the overall corporate climate will continually stifle innovation.

# HOW THINKING ABOUT LEADERSHIP HAS DEVELOPED

Van Seters and Field (1990) have produced a valuable analysis of the stages through which leadership theory has evolved. The first phase they describe as the 'Personality Era', dating, in terms of serious scientific work, from the late nineteenth century and, in particular, the work of Francis Galton. They further subdivide this era into two periods: the

'Great Man Period' and the 'Trait Period'. In the former approach attention focuses on great men and women leaders in history and on their personalities, on the assumption that the route to becoming an effective leader was to study their lives and emulate them. This methodology comes up against two problems: first, the world's most effective leaders – Gandhi, Mandela, Churchill, Thatcher, etc – display widely different personal qualities; and second, studying such a person is one thing, being able to copy one of these would be another altogether. Nevertheless, this approach is still being pursued in the context of business where leaders in the industrial and commercial world such as Jack Welch, Percy Barnevik or John Harvey-Jones take the place of the world's great political leaders.

The 'Trait' approach abandons the attempt to link leadership qualities with particular individuals and involves listing a number of traits which are believed in general to relate to effective leadership. Unfortunately, empirical studies have failed to establish a link between effective leadership and any single trait or group of traits. Despite this, the trait approach is still very much favoured in popular treatments of the subject, as we shall see later.

The second phase of development is characterized as the 'Influence Era'. This recognises that leadership is a process involving relationships between individuals and cannot be understood by focusing solely on the leader. Again this is subdivided into two periods: the 'Power Relations Period' and the 'Persuasion Period'. In the first, explanations are sought in terms of the sources of power and how it is used. In the latter, as the name implies, attention focuses on how the leader achieves domination through the use of skills of persuasion.

The third phase strikes out in a fresh direction by focusing on what leaders actually do – looking at typical leader *behaviour* patterns and differences in behaviour between effective and ineffective leaders. The subdivision here is between the 'Early Behaviour Period' and the 'Late Behaviour Period'. The most well-known work from the former was carried out at Ohio State and Michigan Universities and led to the identification of two important dimensions of leader behaviour: Initiating Structure (or concern for the task) and Consideration (concern for individual satisfaction and group cohesion). During the 'Late Period' these findings were adapted and applied in industry, most notably by Blake and Mouton whose Managerial Grid (see Chapter 5) was adopted as a tool in leadership development by very many industrial enterprises.

Also prominent at this time was the work of Douglas McGregor who drew a distinction between Theory X which holds that people need direction and 'carrot and stick' type incentives if they are to perform well in industrial organizations and Theory Y which holds that people are intrinsically motivated to achieve and need only the opportunity and a supportive working environment.

Phase four has been styled the 'Situation Era' in which researchers turned their attention to the *context* in which leadership is being exercised. There are three subdivisions of this era: the 'Environment Period' focuses on how leaders emerge in the right place at the right time to meet the needs of the hour; the 'Social Status Period' looked at the leaders' and subordinates' mutual expectations of their behaviour; and the 'Socio-Technical Period' (exemplified by the work of the Tavistock Institute in Britain) brought the environmental and social influences together.

The authors describe the fifth phase – the 'Contingency Era' – as 'a major advance in the evolution of leadership theory'. For the first time it was recognized that leadership was not found in any of the pure, unidimensional forms discussed previously, but rather contained elements of them all. In essence, effective leadership was contingent or dependent on one or more of the factors of behaviour, personality, influence and situation. Among the most important contributors to this advance were Fiedler and Vroom. Much of the work falling into this category involves complex models to which practising managers find it very difficult to relate.

The sixth phase, which they call the 'Transactional Era', added to the previous insights the idea that 'leadership resided not only in the person or the situation but also, and perhaps rather more, in role differentiation and social interaction'. In this phase the 'Exchange Period' is characterised by the work of Bass, which emphasizes the importance of transactions between leaders and subordinates and the leader's role in initiating and sustaining interaction. Bass's work is still a respected element in leadership theory.

The 'Role Development Period' refers specifically to the relative roles of leader and subordinate and suggests that leadership can sometimes reside in the subordinate rather than the leader. This era was followed by the 'Anti-Leadership Era'. The idea grew that there was possibly no valid concept called leadership. This era fell into the 'Ambiguity Period' (when it was argued that leadership existed only as a perception in the mind of the observer) and the 'Substitute Period' (which focused on ways in which characteristics of the task and of the organization could act as substitutes for leadership in affecting performance).

The eighth era – the 'Culture Era' – adopted the idea that if a leader can create a strong culture in an organization, then people will in effect lead themselves. The key role of the leader is to recognize the need for culture change and to bring about the necessary changes. The work of such writers as Schein and Peters falls into this group.

Van Seters and Field describe the ninth era – the 'Transformational Era' – as 'the latest and most promising phase in the evolutionary development of leadership theory'. Here the focus is on leader behaviour during periods of organizational transition and on processes such as creating visions of a desired future state and obtaining employee commitment to change. The subdivisions here are into the 'Charisma Period' and the 'Self-Fulfilling Prophecy Period'. The former, as the name indicates, focuses on strong executive leadership which both creates the vision and empowers subordinates to carry it out and is exemplified in the work of Tichy and Devanna. The latter emphasizes the way in which effective transformational leadership involves the building of positive expectations.

The authors of this study summarize their review of the field by stating that researchers need to recognize five aspects of the leadership phenomenon:

1.  That it is a complex process with behavioural, relational and situational aspects.

2.  That it exists, as well as in the leader, in the dyadic, group and organizational relationships.

3.  It can stem from lower organizational levels as well as top-down.

4.  It occurs both internally, in leader-subordinate interactions, and externally, in the situational environment.

5.  That it motivates people intrinsically by improving expectations as well as extrinsically by manipulating reward systems.

This work represents a valiant and competent effort at tracing the development of thinking and research about leadership and is useful in that it does provide a framework into which the various approaches can be fitted. Its weakness, however, lies in its failure to fit and do justice to the key characteristic of the field to which they themselves draw attention – its complexity. As we shall see, there are many approaches – including some extremely helpful ones – which it is difficult to fit into their categories either because they spread over several of them or because they fail to fit with any.

Crainer (1996) using a simpler, less academic way of classifying approaches to the study of leadership, divides the 'schools of thought' on leadership into the following categories:

1.  **Great Man Theories.** Based on the belief that leaders are exceptional people, born with innate qualities, destined to lead. The misleading nature of this approach has already been mentioned.

2.  **Trait Theories.** The lists of traits or qualities associated with leadership exist in abundance and continue to be produced. They draw on virtually all the adjectives in the dictionary which describe some positive or virtuous human attribute, from ambition to zest for life. This approach will be explored in Chapter 3.

3.  **Power and Influence Approaches.** These focus on the exercise of power and influence and assume the centralization of decision making and a passive role for subordinates.

4.  **Behaviourist Theories.** Concentrate on what leaders actually do rather than on their qualities. These ideas are developed in Chapter 4. Different patterns of behaviour are observed and categorized as 'styles of leadership'. This area has probably attracted most attention from practising managers. It is summarized in Chapter 5.

5.  **Situational Leadership.** This approach sees leadership as relatively specific to the situation in which it is being exercised. For example, military leadership may demand skills, qualities and behaviours which differ from those associated with successful leadership in industry or the Church.

6.  **Contingency Theory.** This is a refinement of the situational viewpoint and focuses on identifying the situational variables which best predict the most appropriate or effective leadership style to fit the particular circumstances.

7.  **Transactional Theory.** This approach emphasizes the importance of the relationship between leader and followers, focusing on the mutual benefits derived from a form of 'contract' through which the leader delivers such things as rewards or recognition in return for the commitment or loyalty of the followers.

8.  **Attribution theory.** Here the emphasis is on the power of the followers and the factors which cause them to attribute leadership to a particular person.

9. **Transformational Theory.** The central concept here is change and the role of leadership in envisioning and implementing the transformation of organizational performance.

# SUMMARY

Leadership is an elusive concept, difficult of definition and the definitions offered by different writers in the field differ considerably. The term is sometimes used to refer to an attribute of a person, as in the phrase 'his leadership was exemplary', but is more usefully employed to refer to a social process involving influence and persuasion. As such it involves interaction between people who offer leadership and people who accept the offer and act as followers.

The concept has attracted the attention of a wide range of interested observers from psychologists and sociologists engaged in serious research, through historians to writers of fiction. In the course of time a number of myths have grown up around the topic, such as the assertion that leaders are born, not made, and that leaders are people with charismatic personalities.

One thing is clear. Leadership takes a wide variety of forms depending on the situation. Leading in small face-to-face groups is a different kind of process, involving different kinds of behaviour and different skills compared with leading at the top of a large complex organization. Much research and writing has focused on truly great world-class leaders such as Nelson, Ghandi and Churchill in the past or Kennedy, Thatcher and Welch in modern times. Yet our institutions function as a result of acts of leadership by many, many people who seldom receive recognition.

There are some grounds for believing that progress in leadership studies is being made. Over the years thinking and research has advanced in several ways:

■ from attempts to list the traits of successful leaders to studies of their actual behaviour;

■ from the 'great man' approach to studies of leadership at different levels and in everyday working situations;

■ from a focus on the leader to a focus on the interaction between the leader and followers, and on the situation in which that interaction occurs.

# 2

# Leadership and management

## DISTINGUISHING LEADERSHIP FROM OTHER ROLES

There are at least seven distinct roles concerned with the exercise of power and influence in organizations:

1. **Political office holder**, eg government minister or town mayor. The legitimacy of the authority vested in this role in a democratic society derives from the ballot box. Acceptance of such authority is for the most part willingly given but in the last resort is enforced by the courts. In a democratic society there are safeguards to prevent the arbitrary exercise of the power associated with holding a political office or using that power in a self-interested way.

2. **Commander.** A role confined to military or paramilitary organizations, its legitimacy stems from the nature of the threats to society which the organization exists to deal with, such as the exigencies of war. The commander's orders are backed by the sanctions of stern discipline. Command is not necessarily perfectly correlated with rank. For example the captain of a ship or an aircraft is in command although he may be junior in rank to another officer who may be acting as a member of the crew or in an advisory role.

3. **Administrator or bureaucrat** (in the positive, Weberian, sense). This is the traditional public service role which derives the legitimacy

of its authority from a rational/legal set of rules and regulations and from the holding of an office with defined powers within a structure of authority and control. Challenges to the rules are rare but when they occur the response is procedural and measured. Administrators are judged by their ability to maintain order, stability, uniformity of treatment and impartiality.

4.   **Manager.** The 20th century invention, as ownership of the means of production became separated from control and a new professional managerial class emerged. Its authority is legitimized – at least in theory – by consent of the shareholders. The greatest challenge to managerial authority in the past has come from the labour unions. The traditional sanction has been 'the sack'. Increasingly, however, managerial authority is being challenged by consumers' groups and by groups in the community representing various viewpoints such as animal rights or environmental conservation. In the face of such pressures from outside managerial authority often evaporates rapidly.

5.   **The expert, specialist or professional.** The role which supplies the expertise essential to the decision-making process. The authority which comes from the possession of superior knowledge or professional competence is, perhaps, the least likely to be challenged, although in an industrial and commercial culture such as that in the UK, which places relatively low value on technical expertise, it is in danger of being ignored.

6.   **The entrepreneur.** The one who conceives the organization and brings it into being and whose authority is based on ownership of both the idea and the assets of the business.

**The seventh role is that of the leader.** It differs from the other six in the following ways. First, in the context of organizational life it never exists in isolation – it is always linked in hybrid fashion to some other role, so that we have political leaders, military leadership, administrative leadership, managerial leadership, expert leadership, entrepreneurial leadership or, indeed leadership on the part of a person whose role carries no formal authority such as a shopfloor worker.

Second, for this reason people do not normally choose a career as a leader. People embark upon careers in politics, public service, the armed forces, in industrial management, in one of the professions or decide to start their own business. Whatever choice they make will reflect a complex pattern of motivation, aptitude, expectations and influences from family, education and careers advisers. In this process little attention is normally paid to questions of leadership. The seventh role is an add-on: an afterthought in most cases, with the possible exception of a career in the armed services. Conversely, except when seeking a new chief executive from outside, organizations rarely advertise for leaders when recruiting, and in many cases do not select for leadership potential although this has been changing in recent years.

Once a person has embarked on the career of choice the expectation that he or she should start acting out the role of leader is likely to be very high in the military or paramilitary role, much less strong in other roles and least likely in the administrative role or in that of expert or professional. This means that if we want to develop leaders in industry or the public services there is a lot to be done in changing expectations.

Third, the legitimacy of the leadership role as a source of power and influence is inalienable from the personal qualities and/or actions of the leader. In respect of all the other roles the legitimacy derives from the properties of the office held. We accept the authority of the political office holder or the public official or the works manager or the doctor or the proprietor because of the position held. No chemist when filling a prescription wants to know more about the doctor who signed it. A directive from head office is enacted if the managing director has signed it even if the people at the receiving end have never met the managing director. Leadership, however, is *personal*. We accept leadership or not on the basis of judgements we make about the person offering leadership and these judgements will be based to some extent on what we perceive as his or her personal qualities and to some extent on his or her observable behaviour. A quality frequently mentioned in this context is *charisma* – difficult to define 'but we know it when we see it'. Other perceived qualities, however, may be equally important – ones such as sincerity and integrity or intellect or judgement. These qualities are the ones we perceive; our perception of them is based on a range of observations; what a person says is an obvious source of information, as is how a person behaves, particularly at times of crisis. Being human, however, we also have stereotypes and we are influenced by superficial characteristics of the individual, for instance, height or form of dress. Our stereotype may be more like Russell Crowe in the film *Gladiator* than like a great real life leader such as Nelson Mandela. The qualities we look for will, however, be strongly influenced by our values and the culture of the organization. Workers on a building site will look for and see different qualities from those respected by a group of senior civil servants or the members of a theatre company.

What are the extra ingredients which leadership adds to the performance of other roles in organizations? One answer is, in a word, *motivation*. Those who add the leadership role to their primary role have little or no need to fall back on the sanctions which support their authority. We accept their judgement and follow willingly because we trust their leadership. This trust derives from the extent to which the leader creates a sense of common purpose and a sense of belonging.

A second answer is the *reduction of anxiety*. In times of danger, uncertainty or rapid change people grow anxious, become dependent. They look for leadership as a source of reassurance, as an anchor to provide a degree of security and stability.

## LEADERSHIP AND MANAGEMENT

If one wishes to distinguish leadership from management or administration, one can argue that leaders create and change cultures, while managers and administrators live within them. (Edgar Schein)

Handy (1992) attributes the growing interest in leadership in recent years to an underlying change in the way we think about organizations. He suggests that in the past we thought of organizations as pieces of engineering, 'flawed pieces maybe but capable in theory of perfectibility'. Organizations, thus, were things to be designed, planned and managed. Their effectiveness was to do with control systems and feedback loops.

Today, however, we use a different kind of language when talking about organizations – a language which uses such terms as networks, alliances, culture and shared values. This, Handy argues, is the language of *leadership*, not of management.

Another way of expressing this is that whereas management is a rational process, calling into play abilities such as verbal and numerical reasoning, leadership is more intuitive, involving emotional intelligence.

Cunningham (1986) identifies three different viewpoints on the relationship between leadership and management. The first assumes leadership is one competence among a range required for effective management:

The second, held by Bennis and Nanus (1985) for example, sees the two concepts as separate but related:

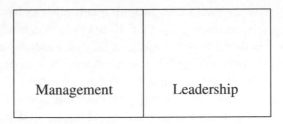

The third sees partial overlap:

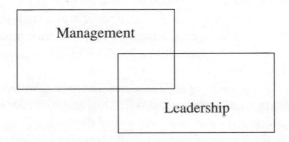

In his 'classic' *Harvard Business Review* article, 'Managers and leaders: are they different?', Zaleznik (1992) dismisses the idea that through training it is possible to develop people to be both effective managers and effective leaders. He argues that they are very different kinds of people, with different motivation, different personal histories and different ways of thinking and acting. He develops his argument under four headings: attitudes towards goals; conceptions of work; relations with others; and senses of self.

For managers, he suggests, *goals* are viewed impersonally, as things arising out of organizational necessities. Leaders, by contrast, adopt a personal approach to goals which reflect their own visions or deeply held beliefs. He gives as an example Edwin Land whose goal to develop the Polaroid camera came from his own personal dreaming and not from any managerial analysis of organizational necessities in meeting customer expectations. (Land, however, fits the role of entrepreneur more closely than that of leader.)

With regard to *work*, he asserts that managers see it as an enabling process which involves a mix of setting strategies, making decisions, planning, negotiating, rewarding and coercing. Managers are concerned with the achievement of acceptable compromise. Leaders 'work in the opposite direction' – they develop fresh approaches to outstanding problems and convey their ideas through images that excite and inspire. To exemplify this, he quotes from J F Kennedy's inaugural, 'Let every nation know, whether it wishes us well or ill, that we shall pay any price, bear any burden, meet any hardship, support any friend, oppose any foe, in order to ensure the survival and the success of liberty'.

*Relations with others*: managers, says Zaleznik, prefer to work with people. He recalls some earlier psychological studies in which managers and other groups were asked to write imaginative stories in response to a picture showing a single figure such as a young boy contemplating a violin. The managers tended to populate their stories with people. At the same time, managers like to maintain a low level of emotional involvement in their relations with others. Leaders interpret such images more emotionally; they relate to people in more intuitive and emotional ways. As a result, leaders generate strong feelings in their followers – both positive and negative.

In discussing the *sense of self*, Zaleznik uses the distinction between personality types put forward by William James in *The Varieties of Religious Experience* – the 'once born' and the 'twice born'. Managers correspond to the former: they are people for whom adjustments to life have been straightforward. Leaders are the 'twice born', their lives marked by a continual struggle to attain a sense of order. Thus managers are suited to the role of perpetuating and strengthening existing organizations and the exercise of duty and responsibility.

Leaders may work in organizations but they never belong to them. Their sense of identity does not depend on formal role or status. Managers are developed through socialization which prepares the individual to preserve the existing order. Leaders are developed through personal mastery which prepares the individual to seek change.

Kotter (1990) puts forward the thesis that management is about dealing with complexity whereas leadership is about coping with change. Management brings order and consistency to complex organizations. It involves planning and budgeting. Leadership is about setting a direction, developing a vision of the future and strategies for achieving the vision. Management is concerned with the achievement of plans through such processes as designing the organization structure and staffing. Leadership is about aligning people – obtaining their commitment to the realization of the vision. Management is about controlling and problem solving, while leadership is about motivating and inspiring.

Kotter emphasizes the difference between organizing people and aligning them. Decisions about organization structure he likens to 'architectural decisions' using the building blocks of jobs, reporting relationships, delegation and control systems. Alignment is mainly about communication – getting the message across to large numbers of people both inside the organization and on the outside and establishing its credibility. Alignment empowers people in two ways: first, when the direction being taken is clear, employees in front-line jobs can take initiatives confident of being supported by their superiors; second, because everyone is pulling together with a common understanding of the overall direction, it is less likely that the initiatives of different members of the organization will be in conflict with each other.

Achievement of a challenging vision calls for the release of energy and this is achieved through motivation and inspiration. Effective leaders motivate people in a number of ways. They express the vision in terms of the values of the people they are leading; they involve people in deciding how to achieve the vision; they provide coaching and feedback; they role-model the vision; and they recognize and reward success.

Adams and Spencer (1986) draw a distinction between a reactive style of thinking and behaviour and a creative style (noting, *en passant*, that the two words are made up of the same letters and that 'the only difference between the two is that you 'C' (see) differently!').

The reactive style involves solving problems quickly, maintaining stability and the *status quo*, reflecting on the past and taking corrective actions after events have taken place, thinking rationally and analytically, breaking things down into their components as a way of understanding them and being controlled by external circumstances.

The creative style, by contrast, focuses on desired outcomes without assuming constraints, relies on intuition a great deal, anticipates events and adopts a preventive approach, takes a systemic perspective – seeing the interrelationships of the parts to the whole – and is characterized by inner control or personal mastery.

The reactive style they regard as the basis for managerial behaviour, while the creative style is the basis for leadership.

According to Clark and Clark (1994), 'Management refers to any system of structure and control that leads to the timely accomplishment of specific tasks within defined resource limits. The chief advantage of leadership behaviour over management practices is the positive effect on group processes and performance'.

Peters (1987), in more robust style talks of the manager as cop, referee, devil's advocate, dispassionate analyst, professional, decision maker, naysayer and pronouncer. Leadership, by contrast, is about being cheerleader, enthusiast, nurturer of champions, hero finder, wanderer, dramatist, coach, facilitator and builder. His role models for leadership are people like Bill Hewlett of Hewlett Packard, Steve Jobs of Apple and Sam Walton of Walmart.

# TRANSACTIONAL AND TRANSFORMATIONAL LEADERSHIP

The distinction between management and leadership is very close to the well-known distinction between *transactional* and *transformational* leadership. This distinction was first made by James McGregor Burns in 1978. Although he was writing about political leadership the distinction has been applied in the sphere of business leadership where it is seen as equally relevant.

Transactional leadership occurs when managers take the initiative in offering some form of need satisfaction in return for something valued by employees, such as pay, promotion, improved job satisfaction or recognition. The manager/leader sets clear goals, is adept at understanding the needs of employees and selects appropriate, motivating rewards.

Transformational leadership, however, is the process of engaging the commitment of employees in the context of shared values and a shared vision. It is particularly relevant in the context of managing change. It involves relationships of mutual trust between leaders and led. Bass and Avolio (1990) suggest that transformational leadership has four components:

1. **Idealised influence.** Having a clear vision and sense of purpose, such leaders are able to win the trust and respect of followers. By showing them they can accomplish more than they believed possible they build a base for future missions which enables them to obtain extra efforts from them.

2. **Individual consideration.** Paying attention to the needs and potential for development of their individual followers. Delegating, coaching and giving constructive feedback.

3. **Intellectual stimulation.** Actively soliciting new ideas and new ways of doing things.

4. **Inspiration.** Motivating people, generating enthusiasm, setting an example, being seen to share the load.

For Burns, transformational leadership involves the maximum amount of mutual interest and the minimum amount of coercion. It always involves restraint in the use of power.

# CHARACTERISTICS OF TRANSFORMATIONAL LEADERS

Tichy and Devanna (1986) having observed a number of transformational leaders in action drew the conclusion that they shared a number of common characteristics that differentiated them from transactional leaders. These were as follows:

▮ They clearly see themselves as *change agents*. They set out to make a difference and to transform the organization for which they are responsible.

▮ They are *courageous*. They can deal with resistance, take a stand, take risks, confront reality.

▮ They *believe in people*. They have well-developed beliefs about motivation, trust and empowerment.

▮ They are driven by a strong set of *values*.

▮ They are life-long *learners*. They view mistakes – their own as well as other people's – as learning opportunities.

▮ They can cope with *complexity, uncertainty and ambiguity*.

▮ They are *visionaries*.

Tichy and Devanna studied 14 business leaders in reaching their conclusions. In almost every case they spent several hours interviewing each person in depth. They selected them on the grounds that they had exhibited successful leadership at different levels of the organization and throughout most of their careers. The work was carried out in the early 1980s and the authors rightly pointed out that it would be the next decade before the extent of their success in transforming their companies could be judged.

The list of those interviewed includes Lee Iacocca, who is often cited as the epitome of the transformational leader. He was fired from his job as president of the Ford Motor Company and joined Chrysler in 1979. At the time he did not know the full extent of the difficulties he was going to have to face. The company was, in fact, on the verge of bankruptcy. He built up a new top management team, firing 35 vice-presidents and hiring 14 former colleagues from Ford, and led the organization through one of the most remarkable turnarounds in the history of US industry. He was able to create a motivating vision of Chrysler's future while simultaneously laying off 60,000 employees. He was as effective in communicating this vision externally to government investors and the banking community as internally to the managers and workers. He also communicated effectively with the unions and with suppliers. He understood that he needed the cooperation of all the stakeholders if Chrysler was to survive.

## MAVERICKS AND CORPOCRATS

Kanter (1992) uses more colourful language to make a distinction similar to that between the transformational and transactional leader. She contrasts two extremes: the conservative resource preserver or 'trustee' and the insurgent entrepreneur or 'promoter'. Other images are, for the former, 'organization man' or 'corpocrat' and for the latter, 'maverick' or 'cowboy'. She points out that although the corpocratic style is on the way out, the maverick is still unsatisfactory as a leadership style, as evidenced by Steve Jobs' problems at Apple.

The tensions between the two styles take several forms. Mavericks want immediate action, corpocratic managers want time to assess the situation and exercise judgement. Mavericks take big 'bet your company' risks. The manager seeks to balance risk and opportunity with safeguarding the core business. Mavericks strain limits whereas corpocrats establish the rules and apply them uniformly. Mavericks motivate largely through personal loyalty whereas corpocrats invoke a more impersonal loyalty to the corporation. Mavericks often reject the trappings and symbols of rank and wealth (Richard Branson's informal dress style is characteristic), whereas corpocrats use them both as a power-base and to motivate others. Kanter calls for a judicious mix of both. Put at its simplest, Kodak needs more mavericks, Apple needs more corporate organization people.

The most well-known exemplar of the maverick type of leader is Ricardo Semler, whose book describing his experiences is titled *Maverick* (Semler, 1993). Semler is president of Semco/SA, a large marine and food processing machinery manufacturer based in Brazil. In his book he sets out his philosophy of business leadership which, seen from the standpoint of orthodox management theory, is radical in the extreme. A basic principle is that the leader's job is to create an environment in which others make decisions. 'Success means not making them myself.' To this end he works from home most mornings; he takes at least two months each year to travel to remote parts of the globe and never calls in, though he does leave a number where he can be reached. One of his first acts as president was to throw out the rule book and replace it with a 20 page booklet called *The Survival Manual*, which has lots of cartoons but few words. Under the heading 'Clothing and appearance', below a cartoon the words state that 'Neither has any importance at Semco. A person's appearance is not a factor in hiring or promotion'.

At the time he wrote his best-selling book in 1993 Semler, aged 34, had been CEO for over 10 years. His unorthodox approach has been highly successful. Semco grew elevenfold between the late 1980s and the early 1990s during which time the Brazilian economy was in deep recession.

Table 2.1 sets out the main differences between leadership and management.

# SUMMARY

One thing is clear: not all managers are leaders. Some managers achieve compliance by the exercise of position power and the use of sanctions; this is not leadership. Similarly, not all leaders are managers, including many who are employed to manage. Managing is about planning, organizing and controlling. It involves dealing with financial and material resources as well as with people. The ideal chief executive is one who combines leadership with the skills and knowledge which a general manager requires.

The distinction between transactional and transformational leadership appears to me to cloud the issue, for two reasons. First, the way the transactional leader is described is very close to the role of the manager rather than the leader and confuses the two roles. Second, the use of the term 'transformational' gives too much emphasis to the role

**Table 2.1** *The manager's world and the leader's world*

| The manager's world | The leader's world |
| --- | --- |
| Exploiting financial, material and human resources (capital, plant and equipment, premises, and labour) | Empowering people; building commitment and alignment with the organization's purpose |
| Contractual relationships with employees, customers and suppliers | Relationships with stakeholders based on mutual trust |
| Key tasks are planning, organizing, directing and controlling | Key tasks are defining purpose, and creating shared vision and values |
| Legitimacy is conferred by virtue of the office held and the authority vested in it | Legitimacy resides in trust based on perceived competence and integrity |

of the leader in bringing about change. Although this aspect of leadership is very much to the fore in today's rapidly changing business environment we should not overlook the important role leadership can play when change is not an issue, for example in persuading a research team to persist with the search for a particular solution to a problem after having experienced several failures or, indeed, in persuading people to resist change.

Practising managers and leaders may find the academics' concern with making these distinctions pretty pointless. It is important, however, for the purpose of selecting and training people to be clear about the nature of the roles they are to play and the qualities which particular roles will require. In the next chapter we look at the perennial question of whether or not leaders possess personal qualities which others do not, at least not to the same degree.

# 3

# Leadership qualities

## LISTS OF QUALITIES

When asked to list the qualities of an effective leader, few people hesitate to reply. We all have our ideas of what it takes. Our ideas do not, however, necessarily overlap a great deal nor do they necessarily agree with the evidence. In 1988 Management Centre Europe surveyed some 1500 top and middle managers across Europe (Syrett and Hogg, 1992). Respondents' replies to the question, 'What qualities does the ideal CEO need?' resulted in five key leadership attributes being identified:

▌ The ability to build effective teams.

▌ The ability to listen.

▌ The capability to make decisions on his (*sic*) own.

▌ The ability to retain good people.

▌ The ability to surround himself (*sic*) with good people.

Asked to list the top five attributes of their own CEOs, respondents' replies resulted in the following list:

▌ Capable of making decisions on his (*sic*) own.

▌ Strong-willed.

▌ Ambitious.

▌ Energetic.

▌ Motivated by power.

Wess Roberts (1992), Vice-President, Human Resources, American Express, is an example of someone who derives his ideas about leadership qualities from his own experience in business. He puts his list of leadership qualities into the mouth of Attila the Hun in an allegorical essay originally published in his book, *The Leadership Secrets of Attila the Hun.* He gives 17 qualities:

▌ Courage.

▌ Desire, ie the strong wish to lead.

▌ Emotional stamina – the ability to persist in the face of disappointment.

▌ Physical stamina.

▌ Empathy – including sensitivity to other people's values and other cultures, beliefs and traditions.

▌ Decisiveness.

▌ Anticipation.

▌ Timing.

▌ Competitiveness.

▌ Self-confidence.

▌ Accountability – in particular, never heaping praise on oneself for one's own achievements or laying blame on others for what one fails to bring about.

▌ Responsibility.

▌ Credibility.

▌ Tenacity.

▌ Dependability.

▌ Stewardship – leaders are custodians of the interests and wellbeing of those they serve as leaders.

▌ Loyalty.

Other writers base their list on research studies of successful business leaders. For example, John P Kotter (1988) of Harvard lists the following 'necessary personal attributes of effective leaders at senior level':

■ Relevant knowledge of products, technologies, markets and people.

■ A keen mind, analytical ability, the capacity to think strategically and 'multi-dimensionally' and sound business judgement.

■ An impressive track record.

■ Sound relationships with key players inside and outside the company.

■ Good interpersonal skills and integrity.

■ Lots of energy.

■ Highly motivated to lead and self-confident.

## CHARISMATIC LEADERSHIP

Bass (1992) quotes Max Weber's view of charisma which has five elements:

■ A person with extraordinary gifts.

■ A crisis.

■ A radical solution to the crisis.

■ Followers attracted to the exceptional person believing that they are linked through him (*sic*) to transcendental powers.

■ Validation of the person's gifts and transcendence in repeated experiences of success.

This pattern sounds very like the transformational leadership described in the previous chapter, but the focus here is on the personal attribute of charisma; this concept of 'extraordinary gifts' and 'transcendent powers'. Bass argues that charisma comes from a combination of emotional expressiveness, self confidence, self determination and freedom from internal conflict. Charismatic leaders are people with a strong conviction in the essential rightness of their own convictions. They are radical, unconventional, risk taking, visionary, entrepreneurial and exemplary. There is an intense emotional attachment to them on the part of their followers which goes beyond such things as trust, respect or admiration to embrace awe, devotion and unswerving loyalty.

Bass has studied charismatic leadership, using a questionnaire instrument, the Multi-factor Leadership Questionnaire (MLQ). He reports that charisma emerged as the most important element in quantitative studies carried out by himself and his colleagues since 1985 in educational institutions, the armed forces, business, industry, hospitals and other non-profit organizations. In the MLQ surveys the following findings emerged:

■ Charismatic leadership was found at all levels in organizations but most often at the top.

■ Many followers described their leaders in terms which indicated charismatic characteristics. Some of these had complete faith in their leaders and were proud to be associated with them.

■ Subordinates who described their immediate superiors as charismatic also rated their units as more productive.

■ Charismatic leaders were seen to be more dynamic. Those working under them had higher levels of self-assurance and saw more meaning in their work.

■ Those working under charismatic leaders worked longer hours.

■ They revealed higher levels of trust in the leader than those working for non-charismatic leaders.

■ High correlations were found between ratings of the charisma of leaders and measures of leadership effectiveness.

Behling and McFillen (1996) have developed a model of the process of charismatic leadership which is based on six attributes of leader behaviour and three beliefs held by followers. The six attributes are derived on the basis of 'good agreement among experts in the field'. They are a mixture of personal qualities and behavioural patterns:

■ Empathy – showing concern for followers' needs, wants and fears.

■ Dramatization of the mission – articulating purpose through compelling, emotive language and through actions.

■ Projecting self-assurance – acting confidently and with certainty.

■ Enhancing own image – creating an impression of personal competence, being a 'winner'.

■ Assuring followers of *their* competence and ability to achieve great things.

■ Providing followers with opportunities to achieve success, delegating responsibility and removing obstacles to followers' performance.

In this model these behaviours on the part of the leader generate or strengthen three important responses on the part of subordinates:

■ Awe – or unreasoning faith in the leader's abilities.

■ Inspiration – followers are persuaded of the moral or ethical purpose of the mission.

■ Empowerment – followers believe they *can* overcome the obstacles and achieve great things.

The authors assert, based on their study of the literature, that the only universally perceived condition necessary for the effective use of charismatic leadership is what they call *psychic distress* – the anxiety related to some kind of crisis or malaise affecting the organization.

## THE WORKING LEADER

Sayles (1993) argues for a less dramatic view of leadership than the conventional picture of the charismatic person able to galvanize followers into action with a compelling vision of a worthwhile goal. He presents the case for the 'working leader': the person who makes the organization work to maximum effect. He answers the challenge, 'Can that be leadership? Isn't that simply what management is all about? Is that so remarkable as to be called leadership?' with an unequivocal, 'Yes!' In his view organizations cannot function effectively without middle managers who can exercise leadership. Leadership skills are needed to overcome the inherent contradictions, bureaucracy and centrifugal tendencies of organizations. 'Almost nothing works without a working leader.'

He defines working leadership as 'the ability to keep adapting, modifying, adjusting and rearranging the complex task and function interfaces that keep slipping out of alignment'.

Drucker (1992) agrees with Sayles. Leadership has little to do with 'leadership qualities' or 'charisma'. It is 'mundane, unromantic and boring' in his opinion. He quotes Eisenhower, George Marshall, Harry

Truman, Konrad Adenauer and Abraham Lincoln as examples of leaders who, while highly effective, possessed 'no more charisma than a dead mackerel'. Moreover, while John F Kennedy was possibly the most charismatic president in US history, 'few presidents got as little done. . .'. Drucker also points out how very different from each other were the great leaders of the Second World War – Roosevelt, Churchill, Eisenhower, Montgomery, Marshall and MacArthur – no two of whom shared any personality traits or qualities.

In Drucker's view, leadership is about work and about performance, beginning with thinking through the organization's mission and articulating it, setting goals and standards. 'The leader's first task is to be the trumpet that sounds a clear sound.' The effective leader, he asserts, is also one who sees leadership as responsibility rather than as rank or privilege. The third requirement according to Drucker is the ability to earn people's trust, which is a function of the leader's integrity and consistency.

More support for the anti-charisma school comes from Binney and Williams (1995). 'Many of the organisations we know do not have charismatic leaders. . . They are usually modest, sometimes even self-effacing, losing no opportunity to stress that real achievement has come from teamwork, not the inspiration of just one individual. Not pretending to be the source of all wisdom, demonstrating some fallibility, is a powerful way of developing commitment to and ownership of issues by others.'

Mintzberg (1999) uses the term 'quiet management' to refer to a non-heroic style of leadership.

> Quiet managers don't empower their people – 'empowerment' is taken for granted. They *inspire* them. They create the conditions that foster openness and release energy. . . Quiet managers strengthen the cultural bonds between people, not by treating them as detachable 'human resources' (probably the most offensive term ever coined in management, at least until 'human capital' came along), but as respected members of a cohesive social system. When people are trusted, they do not have to be empowered.

Quiet managers care for their organization. They spend more time preventing problems than fixing them, because they know enough to know when and how to intervene. Quiet managing is about *infusion*, change that seeps in slowly, steadily. A healthy organization does not have to leap from one hero to another; it is a collective social system that naturally survives changes in leadership. If you want to judge the leader, look at the organization 10 years later.

Quiet leadership works because it is legitimate, meaning that it is an integral part of the organization and so has the respect of everyone there. Indeed, the best managing of all may well be silent. That way people can say, 'We did it ourselves'.

# THE PSYCHOPATHOLOGY OF LEADERSHIP

A number of factors recur in biographical studies which cover the childhood and upbringing of outstanding leaders. One is *isolation*, either in the sense of being separated from other children or the rest of the family or in the sense of being bullied, unpopular or withdrawn. Another is the unsatisfactory nature of the child's *relationships with his or her parents*. A common pattern is an admired, demanding, domineering yet distant father. Another is that of a mother too busy with her career or social life to spend much time with her child. These patterns tend to produce two responses in the individual. One is self-reliance in the sense that he or she is not dependent on the approval of others for his or her actions, does not court popularity and draws on some form of inner strength at difficult times. Another is a strong drive to achieve, to prove oneself, to win, perhaps, the parental approval and applause which was so notably lacking in the earlier years. It is, of course, dangerous and unscientific to draw such conclusions in respect of individual cases but there is considerable statistical evidence that points in this direction.

For example, research by the Institute for Personality Assessment and Research (IPAR); (Ochse 1990), while it does not focus specifically on leadership, has involved in-depth interviews and tests with outstanding achievers in the different fields of activity such as architecture, scientific research, invention and mathematics. People from these fields spent three days living at the Institute, being put under the 'psychological microscope'. It was quite commonly found that the high achievers had suffered traumatic experiences when young, with a high incidence of abuse, illness or deformity. A disproportionate number had lost at least one parent in childhood and social isolation and loneliness, stern discipline and unfair treatment were frequently reported.

Turning to individual instances, the psychiatrist Storr (1969) gives a valuable account of the influences on the development of Winston Churchill. It is, of course, well-known that for most of his life Churchill suffered from chronic depression, a condition he referred to as his 'Black Dog'. Referring to the wartime leader's feat in rallying Britain and raising morale in face of almost certain defeat in 1940, Storr expresses the view that 'only a man who had known and faced despair within himself could carry conviction at such a moment. Only a man who knew what it was to discern a gleam of hope in a hopeless situation, whose courage was beyond reason and whose aggressive spirit burned at its fiercest when he was hemmed in and surrounded by enemies, could have given emotional reality to the words of defiance which rallied and sustained us in the menacing summer of 1940'.

At school, Churchill suffered greatly. His physique was weak with poor muscular development. At preparatory school he was driven to hide among trees to avoid cricket balls thrown at him by other boys. By the time he reached Sandhurst he was only five feet six and a half inches tall and his chest measured a puny 31 inches.

His mother, Lady Randolph Churchill, was only 20 when he was born. A famous society beauty, she had a hectic social life which left her little time for her son. His father was deeply involved in politics. So young Winston received extremely little affection or support from either parent in his early, formative years. Nevertheless, he idolised them both. Storr quotes Violet Bonham Carter as saying, 'Until the end he worshipped on the altar of his Unknown Father'. Storr believes that the hostility Churchill displayed towards school authorities was, in fact, displaced hostility which he could not direct towards his idolized parents. In his early letters from school, Churchill described himself as happy, although he later admitted that this was far from the truth.

Storr goes on to argue that 'intransigent disobedience in the face of authority was young Churchill's only means of self-assertion available at the time, given his physical weakness and a generally poor academic record'. Later in life, however, he discovered a gift which was to play a key role in his eventual success as a leader – a gift with words.

The key qualities which characterized Churchill's leadership and which Storr attributes largely to the circumstances of his early life can be summarized as follows:

■ Outstanding physical courage as a way of compensating for physical weakness and as a means of blotting out memories of early humiliation and bullying.

■ Enormous persistence in the face of setbacks, reflecting his chronic fight against depression.

▌ An extreme drive to achieve reflecting his need to win the approval of his idolized father and adored mother.

It was these characteristics which, when allied with his gift for words and his intuitive and imaginative flow of ideas and with what turned out in the end to be a remarkably robust constitution, enabled him, at a relatively advanced age to lead the nation in its darkest hour.

Another leader whose ability with words lifted the spirits of a great nation was, of course, John F Kennedy. As the second son of one of America's richest men, Jack Kennedy might have been expected to have had an idyllic childhood. Yet his early years were largely solitary, plagued by illness and characterized by rebelliousness in the face of strict parental authority.

The psychoanalytical approach to the study of leadership can be seen in the work of Kets de Vries (1994). He points out that even highly effective leaders of organizations are prone to irrational behaviour and are 'not exactly rational, logical, sensible and dependable human beings'. In his work with business leaders, he attempts to push executives 'to find the deeper meaning behind their actions' and to help them understand that they and their organizations could run into difficulties because of unconscious processes which they find difficult to understand. In order to prepare executives for the painful process of examining the forces behind their own ways of behaving, he gets them to study in some depth the biographies of well-known business leaders. He sets questions such as, 'Why did Henry Ford display behaviour that can only be described as pathological and why, despite this, was he so effective in building a great company based on his vision of the future of the motor car?' He offers a clinical interpretation in terms of Ford's personal history. He was extremely close to his mother but she died when he was only 13. He had a difficult relationship with his father, who strongly disapproved of his choice of a career. He was never able to develop close relationships with other men and had few real friends.

Kets de Vries claims that by gaining insight into the way early relationships and experiences influenced the behaviour of outstanding figures such as Ford, today's business leaders begin to see similar behavioural patterns and personal characteristics in themselves, thus gaining insight into their own motives and enhancing their ability to cope with the exercise of power and authority.

He also uses films such as Arthur Miller's *Death of a Salesman*, Orson Welles' *Citizen Kane* and Ingmar Bergman's *Wild Strawberries* to provide his executives with further insights. Kets de Vries describes what he does as 'neutralising the darker side of leadership' and acknowledges how difficult it can be. Many leaders are not willing to accept the challenge and prefer to remain oblivious to the unconscious forces in their lives.

He points out that through the process known as transference, followers sometimes respond to their leaders as if they were significant figures from the past such as a parent. This results in their displacing their hopes, fears and fantasies on to the leader who then becomes idealized. Leaders with 'a narcissistic disposition' enjoy the consequent admiration and applause but are in danger of becoming unable to function without it. Such leaders can then easily fly into a rage if they meet with resistance or non-compliance. Given the power they have, the effects of these 'tantrums' on the life of the organization can be devastating.

Kets de Vries believes that narcissism and leadership are closely related and that it is an excess of narcissism in leaders which gives rise to egotism and self-centred behaviour. Conditions such as prolonged frustration or disappointment in relationships with parents, or inconsistent or arbitrary behaviour on their part, particularly if linked to violence or abuse, can enhance narcissistic tendencies.

He concludes from his extensive studies of leaders that a considerable percentage have attained leadership roles for what he calls 'negative reasons'. As a result of hardships endured in childhood, they are driven by the need to prove themselves; to strengthen their self-esteem; and to show the world that they are not to be taken lightly.

According to Maccoby (2000), leaders such as Jack Welch and George Soros are examples of productive narcissists; they are gifted and creative strategists who see the big picture and welcome the challenge of changing the world and leaving behind a legacy. 'Indeed, one reason we look to productive narcissists in times of great transition is that they have the audacity to push through the massive transformations that society periodically undertakes.' The danger is that narcissism can turn unproductive when, lacking self-knowledge and restraining anchors, narcissists become unrealistic dreamers. They develop grand schemes and come to believe that only circumstances or enemies block their success. This is the Achilles' heel of narcissists. Because of it, even brilliant narcissists can be suspected of unpredictability, and – in extreme cases – paranoia.

It's easy to see, therefore, why narcissistic leadership doesn't always mean successful leadership. Maccoby cites the case of Volvo's Pehr Gyllenhammar. He had a dream of revolutionizing the industrial workplace by replacing the dehumanizing assembly line caricatured in Charlie Chaplin's *Modern Times*. His vision called for team-based craftsmanship.

Model factories were built and attracted international acclaim. But his success in pushing through these dramatic changes also sowed the seeds for his downfall. Gyllenhammar, Maccoby believes, started to feel that he could ignore the views of his operational managers and pursued risky business deals, which he publicized on television and in the press. 'On one level, you can ascribe Gyllenhammar's falling out of touch with his workforce simply to faulty strategy. But it is also possible to attribute it to his narcissistic personality. His overestimation of himself led him to believe that others would want him to be the czar of a multinational enterprise.' These fantasies led him to pursue a merger with Renault, which was tremendously unpopular with Swedish employees. Because Gyllenhammar was deaf to complaints about Renault, Swedish managers were forced to make their case public. In the end, shareholders rejected Gyllenhammar's plan, leaving him with no option but to resign.

Zaleznik (1998) discusses the way leaders develop as a result of family life and early experiences. He, too, points out that in many instances such trauma as separation from parents, loss of one or more parents or isolation from other children can lead to the development of self-reliance, high achievement, motivation and a degree of self-esteem which is not dependent on externalities. It does not follow that achievement will result, for leaders are like artists in that they struggle with neuroses, their ability to function varies considerably and their self-absorption can be a liability. They are often helped by forming an attachment to a great teacher or other figure who understands them. Zaleznik quotes Eisenhower's relationship with General Connor as a good example of this.

# SUMMARY

The issue of leadership qualities is another example of confusing terminology and confused thinking. The terms personal qualities, traits and attributes are used loosely and with different implications and meanings by different writers. It is useful to make clear a number of distinctions.

First, personal qualities can be divided into five main groups as follows:

■ **Personality traits.** These are the aspects of the individual which come into play in interpersonal relationships. Deriving from the Latin *persona,* meaning mask, our personality is what we present to others with whom we interact. Words like assertive, extrovert, charming or charismatic describe personality. People tend to find some personality traits attractive, others less so. We associate leadership variously with such traits as charisma, presence and self-assurance.

■ **Character.** Unlike personality traits, character is something that one learns about only as a result of knowing a person well over a period of time and observing him or her in a range of situations. It can be defined as the reflection, in a person's behaviour, of his or her basic values. Qualities of character are more often related to leadership qualities than are the more superficial qualities of personality. Ones frequently cited include courage, integrity, sincerity, honesty and persistence.

■ **Temperament.** This aspect of the individual is to do with the emotions. Is the person calm, capable of self control and predictable or erratic and emotionally unstable? We like our leaders, particularly at moments of crisis, to keep their heads and to be able to deal with things calmly and without getting into a state.

■ **Cognitive ability.** It is often asserted that leaders need to be highly intelligent but the evidence for this is not conclusive.

■ **Special Aptitudes or Skills.** These may be relevant in particular fields of activity. For example the leader of a fighter squadron would normally be expected to possess an above average aptitude for flying and to be at least as proficient as his subordinates.

The lists of leadership qualities which various writers offer frequently mix up all these aspects of the individual along with behavioural traits and portmanteau phrases, such as 'the ability to motivate people' which is simply another way of saying 'leadership'.

These are all qualities which are determined by the twin influences of nature and nurture. It is futile to try to answer the question whether Churchill would have emerged as a world-class leader if he had had a happy childhood. People still speak loosely of 'born leaders' when two things are quite clear from the research. First, whatever qualities people may carry with their genes there is a great deal of evidence which shows that such things as achievement drive are greatly influenced by the individual's early upbringing and experiences. Second, as we shall see later there is equally strong evidence that effective leadership behaviour is capable of being developed by various means such as coaching and mentoring, in much the same way that natural ability in athletics can be developed.

As will be made evident later, there is much more to leadership than a set of personal qualities. Nevertheless, it would be wrong to go to the other extreme and to maintain that the study of the personal qualities of effective leaders is sterile. The sheer force of personality or charisma can be seen at work in cases such as Adolf Hitler, John F Kennedy, Charles de Gaulle and Winston Churchill. The qualities approach can be valuable if it is seen as simply one of a whole range of approaches to an enormously complex issue. Its utility will grow to the extent that we are able to measure these qualities and, above all, to gain a better understanding of how they develop.

# 4

# Leader behaviour

It is generally agreed that we stand to learn more about the nature of effective leadership and how to develop leaders by studying the actual behaviour of successful leaders than by trying to find out what special qualities they possess.

## THE VIEWS OF PRACTITIONERS

Several researchers have approached the issue of effective leader behaviour by interviewing practitioners and obtaining their views. Bennis and Nanus (1985) conducted interviews with 90 outstanding leaders, 30 from the public sector and 60 corporate CEOs. They identified four strategies or 'areas of competency':

1.  Attention through vision.

2.  Meaning through communication.

3.  Trust through positioning – being predictable, making your position clear, keeping at it.

4.  Positive self-regard.

Bruce (1986) of the Center for Creative Leadership, interviewed 13 CEOs after retirement. He concluded that leadership at the top involved two main activities: setting the tone of the organization; and setting the direction.

Kotter (1998) of Harvard interviewed 150 managers from 40 firms and obtained the views of nearly 1000 senior executives by means of questionnaires. He also studied leadership in 15 corporations with reputations for good management and in five corporations involved in organizational change. He concluded that effective leadership behaviour in complex organizations has two major dimensions:

1.  Creating an agenda for change. A vision of what can and should be and a strategy for achieving it.

2.  Building a strong implementation network.

Farkas and Wetlaufer (1996) report a study of how chief executives lead based on interviews with 160 chief executives from various countries, most of whom were heading up major enterprises. The aim of the research was to identify the attitudes, activities and behaviours of the executives and to look at similarities and differences in approach. The researchers concluded that there were five distinct approaches, reflecting the relative importance given by the executives to different aspects of the role. One finding was that in effective companies, CEOs did not just approach the leadership role in a way which suited their personalities or personal preferences but tended instead to adopt an approach which best fitted the needs of the organization and its business situation. The five approaches were as follows:

▮ **The Strategy Approach.** These CEOs concentrated on creating and implementing the firm's long-term strategy, spending the greater part of their time dealing with issues outside the firm such as customers, competitors, market trends and technological developments. They delegated the day-to-day operation of the business to senior colleagues. The authors give the CEOs of Coca-Cola and Dell Computer as examples of this style.

▮ **The Human Assets Approach.** These CEOs believe that strategy formulation is a task that should be carried out in the business units, close to the markets, rather than at the centre. They see the CEO's role as imparting a set of values to the organization and influencing attitudes and behaviours. They spend a great deal of time travelling, meeting people and on human resource activities such as recruiting, performance reviews and career development. In other words, they focus on the development of the 'cultural glue' of the company. Examples include the CEOs of Gillette, Pepsi-Co. and Southwest Airlines.

I **The Expertise Approach.** Those who fall into this category focus on developing the company's expertise as a basis for competitive advantage. They therefore spend most of their time on technical matters such as keeping abreast of new technology, analysing competitors' products and ascertaining customer requirements. They cite the CEOs of Motorola and the advertising agency Ogilvy and Mather. (In the latter case, the expertise on which the CEO concentrates is the development and exploitation of brands.)

I **The Box Approach.** Farkas and Wetlaufer use this term to describe the behaviour of the CEO who pays most attention to the development of ways of ensuring control: the controls used are not necessarily or exclusively financial – they could take the form of cultural norms – but the purpose is to ensure uniformity and predictability of employee behaviour and to provide customers with a consistent standard of product or service. These CEOs spend much of their time reviewing regular reports on such matters as financial results or levels of customer satisfaction. They also pay a lot of attention to developing detailed prescriptive procedures. Companies they perceived as being led by CEOs of this type included HSBC Holdings, the NatWest Group and British Airways.

I **The Change Approach.** These CEOs see their job as acting as change agents. Consequently, they spend the greater part of their time communicating the need for change and creating a climate within the organization which accepts continuous change as the natural order of things. John Harvey-Jones, who is profiled in Chapter 9, exemplified this approach when in the top job at ICI. The authors of the article give the CEOs of Tenneco and Goldman Sachs as examples.

The researchers point out that there is, of course, some overlap with CEOs using more than one approach but that the data suggest that in most cases one of the five is clearly dominant.

Hodgson and White (2001) look at leadership from four perspectives:

I **View 1: The economic and strategic view.** The leader has to understand what the strategic need really is in the organization. In more practical terms, the leader will ask 'What is the organization currently trying to do?' and if that doesn't seem like a good idea, then 'What should the organization be trying to do?' The effective leader is looking for a good fit between what the organization can do and become, and what constraints and opportunities there are in the environment in which it operates. The leader may also tackle organizational blind spots by encouraging the organization to gather new or different data so that it can spot market trends earlier.

▌ **View 2: The internal culture.** The leader takes one of three stances that fits the cultural need of the organization:

– *Command and control.* The leader believes in controlling uncertainty because he or she has the expertise, knows what the organization should be doing and know how to do it. In the organization itself, expertise is usually highly valued, and executives are expected, as they rise within the system, to know more than those beneath them do about how things happen.

– *Empowerment.* Here the leader knows what the overall aim (often expressed as a vision) of the organization should be, and controls uncertainty because the organization has groups of people who can come up with the necessary solutions to problems along the way. The leader has to empower the staff in order that they can apply their skills and abilities to the problems ahead. The vision may well be very challenging, but is within the competence of the overall organization.

– *Difficult learning.* This is the paradigm with the greatest degree of uncertainty, and where uncertainty is most likely to be acknowledged. The leader deals with that uncertainty as an evolving, continuous process of discovery, and learning may challenge existing concepts and require genuinely original solutions (our definition of difficult learning). Here the leader's job may be to take the organization towards the things it doesn't know, in search of fruitful areas of confusion and uncertainty, which if conquered would lead to competitive advantage. Through difficult learning, the organization is able to do things that neither it nor its competitors could do before. This leads to competitive advantage.

▌ **View 3: The leader's overall aims.** This is to do with what overall aims leaders have and what their role should be in helping the organization achieve its strategic aims. Aims could range from a safe pair of hands at one end of the scale to the revolutionary at the other. The effective leader has to adopt a role and take necessary actions consistent with furthering the long-term aims. The fit between aim and need is crucial to effectiveness.

▌ **View 4: Knowledge skills and abilities.** Effective leaders will ask themselves what skills they need to help the organization achieve its aims as understood at the three previous levels. There is a wide range of competencies that are appropriate here.

## 'Leaderabilities'

The Ashridge Inventory of Management Skills core list of management competencies contains 29 items describing leadership. (Hind, 2001). These are essentially descriptions of behaviours thought to be associated with leadership and include:

▌ defines and sets high standards of performance/goals for self and others;

▌ encourages others to perform to the highest level;

▌ takes a firm position and stands own ground;

▌ acts decisively and with authority.

Using the data from a sample of over 800 managers, their self-responses on the leadership items were analysed along with the responses from their bosses, subordinates and peers. When the reliability and validity of the statements were considered statistically, it was found that only 11 of them were providing information which reliably distinguished between individuals and provided valid descriptions of behaviours that were agreed to represent leadership in a wide variety of organizations. The other items were not considered reliable or valid for a variety of reasons including too many people being scored too similarly on the behaviour, suggesting that there was some ambiguity or lack of clarity in the wording.

Distilling down the key dimensions of leadership behaviour generates a three-tier model of essential abilities for effective leadership. Leaders must have:

▌ the knowledge abilities to clarify personal goals, and to identify different ways to achieve them through an understanding of the situation – this is directed towards the self and is to do with self and situational awareness;

▋  the process abilities to communicate and enthuse others – this ability is directed towards others and is to do with understanding their goals, needs and abilities;

▋  the facilitative abilities to allow others to perform and achieve autonomously – this is to do with letting others take their own control of achieving the identified goals.

(This research has also examined the accuracy of the ratings made by bosses, peers and subordinates. The results indicate that an awareness of how subordinates in particular, are perceiving and evaluating leadership behaviours is important in effective leadership. Thus leaders should take care to seek feedback from their direct reports at frequent intervals. It has been suggested that transformational leaders – those individuals who encourage real empowerment in their groups through charisma, inspirational motivation, intellectual stimulation and individualized consideration – are more likely to seek feedback from colleagues and to be concerned with the needs of staff.)

## A COGNITIVE APPROACH TO LEADERSHIP

Gardner (1996), a distinguished American psychologist, in his recent work *Leading Minds* has developed what he describes as a *cognitive* approach to the subject. He analyses the characteristics of a number of world class leaders such as Margaret Thatcher, Martin Luther King and Gandhi, including one industrialist in his sample – Alfred P Sloan of General Motors.

He defines leaders as 'persons who, by word and/or personal example, markedly influence the behaviours, thoughts, and/or feelings of a significant number of their fellow human beings'.

Gardner suggests that leaders achieve their effectiveness mainly through the stories they relate and which they embody through the way they live their lives. He distinguishes three levels of leadership:

▋  **The ordinary leader.** This leader simply relates the traditional story of the group in a highly effective way. Examples are Gerald Ford and Georges Pompidou.

▋  **The innovative leader.** This leader brings a new twist to an old story. Thatcher, de Gaulle and Reagan focused on themes that had existed in the past but had been neglected.

■ **The visionary leader.** This individual creates a new story. Gandhi and Monnet are given as illustrations.

For Gardner the arena in which leadership takes place is the human mind – the mind of the leader and the minds of the followers. He argues that the personality of the leader cannot provide an adequate explanation of the success the leader achieves. To understand this we must study the mental structures activated in leaders and their followers. He suggests four factors that are crucial to effective leadership:

■ **A tie to the audience.** An ongoing, active and dynamic relationship between leader and followers.

■ **A certain rhythm of life.** It is particularly important that this should include time for solitary reflection.

■ **An evident link between stories and their embodiment.** The leader must act out the ideas as well as convey them in words.

■ **The centrality of choice.** That is to say, the leader leads by his or her choice and with the consent of the led.

## THE 'VISION THING'

Charles Handy (1992) associates effective leader behaviour with the ability to develop a vision. He sets out five conditions which, in his view, need to be met if visionary leadership is to be effective.

■ First, the vision has to be different. 'A vision has to "reframe" the known scene, to reconceptualise the obvious, connect the previously unconnected, dream a dream.'

■ Second, the vision must make sense to others. It should be seen as challenging, but capable of achievement.

■ Third, it must be understandable and capable of sticking in people's minds. Colin Marshall's vision for British Airways – to become 'the world's favourite airline' – is an example.

■ Fourth, the leader must exemplify the vision by his or her own behaviour and evident commitment.

■ Finally, the leader must remember that if the vision is to be implemented it must be one that is shared.

Kotter (1998) does not share Handy's view that a vision needs to be original and 'different'. In his view, effective business visions are often almost mundane, usually consisting of ideas that are already well-known. He cites as an example the well-known case of Jan Carlzon whose vision was to turn Scandinavian Airlines into the best airline in the world for the business traveller. He did not say anything that was not already common knowledge in the airline industry. The point was that until that time, no airline had taken what was known about the business traveller market and implemented this knowledge effectively.

Kotter asserts that what matters about a vision is not its originality but rather how well it meets the needs of key stakeholders – customers, employees and shareholders – and how easily it can be turned into a strategy which improves the organization's competitiveness.

In the view of Collins (1996) vision is one of the least understood – and most overused – terms in the language.

> Executives spend too much time drafting, wordsmithing, and redrafting vision statements, mission statements, values statements, purpose statements, aspiration statements, and so on. They spend nowhere near enough time trying to align their organizations with the values and visions already in place.
>
> Studying and working closely with some of the world's most visionary organizations has made it clear that they concentrate primarily on the process of alignment, not on crafting the perfect 'statement'. Not that it is a waste of time to think through fundamental questions like, 'What are our core values? What is our fundamental reason for existence? What do we aspire to achieve and become?' Indeed, these are very important questions – questions that get at the vision of the organization.

Vision, he argues, is simply a combination of three basic elements:

▌ an organization's fundamental reason for existence beyond just making money (often called its mission or purpose);

▌ its timeless, unchanging core values; and

▌ huge and audacious – but ultimately achievable – aspirations for its own future.

Of these, the most important to great, enduring organizations are their core values.

Collins points out that the founders of great, enduring organizations like Hewlett-Packard, 3M, and Johnson & Johnson often did not have a vision statement when they started out. They began with a set of strong basic values and a most remarkable ability to translate these into actual behaviours. He cites 3M, a company that has always stuck to its values, promoting innovation, protecting the creative individual, and solving problems in a way that makes people's lives better:

> But what really set 3M apart was the ability of its leadership over the years to create mechanisms that bring these principles to life and translate them into action. For example, 3M allows scientists to spend 15 percent of their time working on whatever interests them, requires divisions to generate 30 percent of their revenues from new products introduced in the past four years, has an active internal venture capital fund to support promising new ventures, preserves a dual career track to encourage innovators to remain innovators rather than become managers, grants prestigious awards for innovations and entrepreneurial success, and so on.

Deering, Dilts and Russell (2002) present the findings of their research and conclude that the successful leader excels in three separate, but related, dimensions. They need to be able to detect and respond to 'weak signals' to 'get ahead of the curve'. They need to achieve congruence in their values and desires and in those of others. And they need to be able to make things happen.

The key role of values is emphasized several times. Successful leaders tend to be more aware than others of their values and beliefs, and make efforts to reflect these in their behaviour. They wear their values and beliefs on their sleeves. Values unite a company around its purpose and vision and conformity with stated values and actual practices are pivotal to an organization's success. 'Successful leaders embody their goals, and align all their beliefs, values, competencies and behaviours behind their 'calling as human beings, rather than merely as business leaders'.

> The leader has to have a moral agenda. If the leader is only saying we want to be the biggest or the most profitable company in the world, forget it. When you do that, there's no leadership. There's nothing more to aspire to. But if your aspirations come from the values of your culture or church or temple or mosque, you have something beyond your own livelihood creation. You're coming to work not as a nine-to-five sort of death but a nine-to-five sort of living. Leaders have to lay out a concept and see what their amazing group of people can do. It's not just about compassion, it's about meaningful accomplishment.
>
> Anita Roddick (2000)

Westley and Mintzberg (1989) identify five distinct styles of visionary leadership.

1.  **The creator** – exemplified by Edwin Land, inventor of the Polaroid camera (and, in the UK, Clive Sinclair?). This type of visionary is characterized by two qualities: originality and the sudden, holistic quality of the vision (akin to a religious experience). Land developed a complete mental picture of his revolutionary camera and how it would work in the space of a few hours. Land, however, would seem to fit into the entrepreneur category rather than be regarded as an exemplary leader.

2.  **The proselytiser** – exemplified by Steven Jobs of Apple. Jobs' contribution to Apple was not so much in the design of the machines – which was more the role of his partner Woznick – as in his evangelical zeal to bring home to people the value and usefulness of the product. He had uncompromising ideas about what kind of organization Apple Computers should be as well as what sort of products it should produce. Richard Branson of Virgin fits into this category.

3.  **The idealist** – exemplified by René Lévesque, leader of the Parti Quebecois. The idealist is one who 'dreams of perfection and minimizes or ignores the flaws and contradictions of the real'. Westley and Mintzberg point out that this type of visionary leader is rarely found in business organizations but in the UK Anita Roddick, founder of the Body Shop, fits the model quite well.

4.  **The bricoleur** – exemplified by Lee Iacocca. The term bricoleur refers to one who frequents junkyards and collects bits and pieces which he puts together to make new objects. Westley and Mintzberg use it to convey the myth-making capacity of some visionary leaders and their ability to build teams, organizations or ideologies and, in particular, the way Iacocca developed the Ford Mustang which was a recombination of 'classic' stylistic elements fitted on to existing car platforms and existing engines. Perhaps John Harvey-Jones is the UK leader who best fits this category, particularly in the light of his ability to create myths and weave legends.

5.  **The diviner** – exemplified by Jan Carlzon. The diviner's key quality is insight into such processes as how to build an organization. Carlzon displayed such insights into the nature of service and the type of organizational structure most likely to deliver it. The UK equivalent must surely be Colin Marshall.

In the UK, the Eden Project – the creation of two vast biodomes in a disused china clay quarry – provides a superb example of vision translated into action. In the words of the project's initiator, Tim Smit, 'Eden isn't so much a destination as a place in the heart. It is not just a marvellous piece of science-related architecture, it is also a statement of our passionate belief in an optimistic future for mankind.' The achievement of Smit's vision called for it to be shared by a large team of specialists in areas of expertise ranging from drainage systems to long-term finance; it required an act of faith and the will to overcome seemingly insurmountable obstacles; it involved a set of shared values summed up in one word: stewardship.

> We are also here to show that environmental awareness is about the quality of life at all levels. The environment is shorthand for issues that impact on us in a thousand ways every day, from the food that we eat and the clothes that we wear to the weather we enjoy or suffer. Most of all we wanted Eden to be a symbol of what is possible when people put their mind to the challenge of regeneration and restoration.

## FORTHRIGHT LEADERSHIP

Binney and Williams (1995) describe effective leaders as ones who both lead and learn – leading from a confident 'knowing' position and being willing at the same time to be open to challenge and new ideas. These leaders, they assert, have four characteristics:

- **Operational credibility.** This is a function of having a deep understanding of the business, its products and the issues to do with it.

- **Being 'connected' to their organizations.** Being in close touch with employees and customers.

- **Leading by example.** If leaders practise 'Do as I say' rather than 'Do as I do', they will fail to be effective.

- **Consistency under pressure.** For example, in being willing to communicate bad news as well as good news.

Binney and Williams use the term 'forthright leadership' to describe a type of leader who is frank, direct and prepared to go out on a limb for the things they believe in. They are not held back by convention, tradition or bureaucracy and are willing to risk their personal reputation and career.

It is this combination of forthright leadership with the willingness to listen and learn which is powerful and effective. Leaders should ensure that there is clarity about the direction and objectives but, in the context set by that direction, should give space, time and knowledge so that people can exercise initiative.

## Leading change

Kanter (1999) reports the following behaviours as characteristic of leaders who successfully manage change:

1.  **Tuning in to the environment.** A leader can't possibly know enough, or be in enough places, to understand everything happening outside the organization. But they can actively collect information that suggests new approaches, for instance by paying special attention to customer complaints, which are often the best source of information about an operational weakness or unmet need. Also it is important to search out broader signs of change – a competitor doing something differently or a customer using a product or service in unexpected ways.

2.  **Challenging the prevailing organizational wisdom.** Leaders need to develop what Kanter calls 'kaleidoscope thinking' – a way of constructing patterns from the fragments of data available, and then manipulating them to form different patterns. Leaders should question existing assumptions about how pieces of the organization, the marketplace or the community fit together.

3.  **Communicating a compelling aspiration.** A leader cannot sell change without genuine conviction. Especially when pursuing a true innovation as opposed to responding to a crisis, it is vital to make a compelling case.

4.  **Building coalitions.** Change leaders need the involvement of people who have the resources, the knowledge and the political clout to make things happen.

5.  **Transferring ownership to a working team.** Once a coalition is in place, the leader can enlist others in its implementation. The leader's job is to support the team, provide coaching and resources, and give it a sense of ownership.

6.  **Learning to persevere.** One of the mistakes leaders make in change processes is to launch them and leave them.

7. **Making everyone a hero.** Recognizing, rewarding and celebrating accomplishments is a critical leadership skill, and it is probably the most under-utilized motivational tool in organizations.

John Kotter (1998), having studied more than 100 companies, found that successfully leading change involved eight critical steps:

1. Establish a sense of urgency:

   ▌ examine market and competitive realities;

   ▌ identify and discuss crises, potential crises and major opportunities.

2. Form a powerful guiding coalition:

   ▌ assemble a group with enough power to lead the change effort;

   ▌ encourage the group to work as a team.

3. Create a vision:

   ▌ create a vision to help direct the change effort;

   ▌ develop strategies for achieving that vision.

4. Communicate the vision:

   ▌ use every vehicle possible to communicate the new vision and strategies;

   ▌ teach new behaviours by the example of the guiding coalition.

5. Empower others to act on the vision:

   ▌ get rid of obstacles to change;

   ▌ change systems or structures that seriously undermine the vision;

   ▌ encourage risk taking and non-traditional ideas, activities and actions.

6. Plan for and create short-term wins:

   ▌ plan for visible performance improvements;

   ▌ create those improvements;

   ▌ recognize and reward employees involved in the improvements.

7.  Consolidate improvements and produce still more change:

    ▌ use increased credibility to change systems, structures and policies that don't fit the vision;

    ▌ hire, promote and develop employees who can implement the vision;

    ▌ reinvigorate the process with new projects, themes and change agents.

8.  Institutionalize new approaches:

    ▌ articulate the connections between the new behaviours and organizational success;

    ▌ develop the means to ensure leadership development and succession.

## LEGITIMIZING LEADERSHIP

Sayles (1993) has tackled the issue of how leaders make their role legitimate in the eyes of their followers.

1.  By demonstrating superior ability – not necessarily technical skill – and also 'organizational sophistication'.

2.  By demonstrating their knowledge of the norms, expectations and values of the group by, in effect, role-modelling these. (One difficulty facing leaders coming from outside is that they do not know these 'rules of the game'. They may have to depend for guidance on trusted lieutenants who know them well.)

3.  By acting as the group's protector, spokesperson and representative with powerful external forces such as the City, group head office, the unions, the press, etc. 'Nothing legitimates and substantiates the position of leaders more than their ability to handle external relations.' To be effective in this role calls for courage as well as powerful advocacy skills.

4.  By the process of being 'anointed'. A leader can be authenticated by being seen to be held in high regard by someone who is already seen as a great leader. An obvious example is when the leader of a political party endorses a local candidate by appearing on the same platform with him or her.

5.  By maintaining an appropriate measure of 'social distance', the status gap between leader and follower. In today's society we are poised uneasily between a past tradition in which trappings of office were used to emphasize considerable social distance and a more modern set of values which emphasizes egalitarianism. Thus, today's effective leader in business will make it known that he expects people to address him or her by the first name, will leave the office door open, will eat in the same cafeteria as other employees and park in a general parking lot but, at the same time, the respect others have for him or her may be strengthened rather than weakened by the fact that he or she drives a BMW 7 series.

6.  By providing clarity in respect of goals, helping people to focus their energies and make sense of what is going on.

7.  By providing help in solving followers' problems (ones relating to the job and personal ones).

8.  By showing persistence. We admire people who never give up. Leaders who persevere, who insist that their legitimate demands be met, will win respect, however grudging.

9.  By displaying self-confidence. 'Would be leaders who whine, who scold, who plead, are communicating their presumption that subordinates will not do what is being asked'.

10.  By getting things done. This factor can be seen best when it is lacking and people start complaining about the way things are left to stagnate, about 'leadership vacuum' and the need for someone to take responsibility.

11.  By successfully handling challenges to leadership.

In the context of organizational life, challenges to leadership are rarely direct and confrontational. They are usually more subtle. It is not difficult to find plausible reasons for not going along with the leader's suggestions or requests, ie lack of time, shortage of resources, some other department's failure to cooperate, etc. Nevertheless, such challenges can become a crucial test of the leader's credibility. One successful challenge, of course, will soon be followed by others.

Sayles recommends dealing with challenges to leadership by starting with an enquiry rather than a request. 'Through a process of give and take, managers should seek to learn the needs and objectives of subordinates as they relate to the refusal to respond to a request.' Leaders should seek first to reach agreement with the subordinate that there is a problem, should try to understand the employee's viewpoint; and should then try to redefine the problem in such a way that the employee can contribute to its solution. The solution, Sayles argues, then becomes the result of the leader's ability to restructure the problem and at the same time to encourage a parallel restructuring on the part of the employee.

## HOW LEADER BEHAVIOUR INFLUENCES CORPORATE CULTURE

Schein (1992) suggests that there are six what he calls 'primary embedding mechanisms' through which leaders create the 'climate' of an organization and thus lay the foundations of a corporate culture. The first consists of what leaders are seen to pay attention to, to measure and to control. If this is done consciously it forms a very powerful way of putting a message across, especially if the leader behaves in a way that is consistent with it. On the other hand, if the leader does this unconsciously there is the danger of a discrepancy arising between what he or she says is important and what he or she is seen as treating as important.

The second mechanism is the reaction the leader displays in respect of critical incidents or organizational crises. On such occasions the behaviour of the leader reveals such things as assumptions about the importance of people and about the place of praise and blame in motivating employees.

Third, climate is influenced by the criteria the leader is seen to employ in resource allocation. This involves not only the way the budget is allocated across different activities but also the process through which the budget is drawn up, ie top down or bottom up.

The fourth mechanism consists of deliberate role modelling by leaders, using their own visible behaviour to communicate values and assumptions. Schein describes one CEO who believed that status and hierarchy were barriers to communication and innovation. His way of tackling the problem was to drive a small car, have a plain simple office, dress informally and spend many hours walking about the company talking to employees at all levels.

The fifth mechanism is the way in which the leader allocates rewards and punishments. Too many leaders behave inconsistently, exhorting managers, for example, to develop their people and ensure their own personal development, yet rewarding them exclusively on short-term bottom-line results.

The final mechanism consists of the criteria the leader is seen to employ in the processes of recruitment, selection, promotion and 'out-placement'. Leaders run the danger that they are attracted by candidates who resemble themselves in style, assumptions, beliefs and values.

Schein also sets out a list of 'secondary articulation and reinforcement' mechanisms which, in his view, are the reinforcers rather than the creators of culture. They can, however, become primary factors in perpetuating a culture once established and can then act as powerful obstacles to change when new leaders arrive and desire to change the existing culture. These 'secondary mechanisms' include:

▌ **The organization structure.** Leaders, particularly founders of companies, often have very strong theories about how to organize for maximum effectiveness. Colonel Johnson of Johnson & Johnson, with his unshakeable belief in maximum decentralization is a good example.

▌ **Systems and procedures.** These arise out of early actions on the part of the leader and become built in to the life of the organization as a powerful symbol of underlying values.

▌ **Design of the physical environment.** Choices made under this heading can also reinforce the leader's messages, for example, choosing an open office layout.

▌ **Stories about important events and people.** Leaders cannot always control what others will say about them in stories but they can repeat stories about which they feel good.

▌ **Formal statements of philosophy, values or ideology.**

# PRESCRIPTIONS

Quite distinct from the attempts, using various methods, to determine the behaviour patterns of effective leaders are the prescriptions offered by experts and 'gurus' who say, in effect, 'if you want to be a good leader this is what you should do'. The problem this raises is the familiar one that there are as many prescriptions as experts. In recent years one of the most popular 'prescribers' has been Tom Peters. What follows is a summary of his particular recipe (Peters, 1992). The least that can be said about it is that it reflects a lot of experience and reflection on his part and is probably as good as anyone else's. It will certainly serve well as an example of its type.

Peters' prescription involves ten behaviours which he groups under five headings:

■    The guiding premiss – mastering paradox.

■    Tools for establishing direction – developing an inspiring vision, managing by example and practising visible management.

■    Empowering people – listening, deferring to the front line, delegating and 'bashing bureaucracy'.

■    Evaluating people on their 'love of change'.

■    Creating a sense of urgency.

*Mastering paradox* is about being flexible and coping with uncertainty, living with such paradoxes as being competitive while learning to cooperate, combining tighter control with greater decentralization.

*Developing the vision* involves soul-searching, assessment of threats and opportunities, soliciting others' views. The vision should be simultaneously succinct, clear and exciting, yet broad enough to leave considerable scope to pursue new opportunities as they arise.

*Managing by example.* Peters recommends that leaders should spend no less than 50 per cent of their time, visibly and directly, on their top priority. They should try to influence every promotion so as to ensure that promotions are in line with the strategy and the vision. Leaders should pause and consider the symbolic message given by every action on their part.

*Practising visible management* is simply about walking the job, spending time out of the office, being seen.

*Listening* involves much more than being passive. It is about going into things in detail, asking questions, really listening to the answers and then doing something to improve the situation.

*Deferring to the front line* is about showing that you see the front-line people – the ones who make the product or meet the customer – as the organization's real heroes.

*Effective delegation* is not easy. It involves really letting go and not unthinkingly taking back.

Peters loves what he calls 'bashing bureaucracy'. He advocates not letting one day pass without engaging in at least one act of bureaucracy destruction, ie doing things like refusing to read reports longer than two pages.

In relation to *creating a climate favourable to change* he suggests challenging managers and asking them to point to some specific change they have brought about during a working day. If they cannot do this, he argues, they have not earned their pay cheque.

Under the heading *creating a sense of urgency* he makes a number of practical suggestions such as cut out the trappings of office, give up executive perks and be the first to get into work.

# SUMMARY

From these researches emerges a picture of effective leader behaviour, or at least of what is seen to be effective behaviour in a Western, primarily American, context and judged primarily by academics. The good leader tends to share decision making and share responsibility. He or she gives equal emphasis to structuring the task and to showing consideration for subordinates. The good leader is a visionary but is able to develop a shared vision with his or her followers. The good leader is concerned with values and expresses and personifies the values of the group in his or her behaviour. Other key behaviours are:

- Behaving consistently, being predictable.

- Persistence in the face of obstacles or setbacks.

- Communicating, telling stories, but also listening and learning.

- Innovating.

- Solving problems.

- Capable of following through and implementing.

- Being connected to the group and in close touch with what is going on. Walking the job.

- Displaying self-confidence.

- Delegating and empowering.

- Acting as the group's representative and protector.

# 5

# Styles of leadership

Each of us has to develop our own style and our own approach, using such skills and personal qualities as we have inherited. (John Harvey-Jones)

## AUTOCRATIC AND DEMOCRATIC STYLES

Most subsequent work in respect of styles of leadership has been based on two early studies. One of these on behaviour was carried out in 1939 and 1940 by two American researchers, White and Lippitt (1959), and is now regarded as one of the classical experiments in social psychology. Their aim was to evaluate the effectiveness of different ways of exercising the leadership role. In their first experiment they compared two contrasting ways of behaving or styles of leadership – the *autocratic* and the *democratic*. These terms largely speak for themselves; the autocratic leader takes decisions and imposes them on the group, expecting group members to put them into effect without questioning the reasons for them. The democratic leader, on the other hand, encourages the members of his or her group to share the decision taking process and sees him- or herself as a coordinator of group effort, rather than as the decision taker. In a subsequent experiment a third style was also examined which was described as *laissez-faire*. This third type of leader, as the use of the term indicates, plays a passive role in group affairs, and normally interacts with group members only on their initiative.

In this second study four groups of 11-year old boys were formed, matched as far as possible in terms of their personal characteristics and interests. Four adults were then procured to act as leaders to these groups of boys. Each adult was coached so that he could convincingly perform each of the three leadership styles being studied. The groups were then given tasks to do and worked successively under each of the four adults three times, with each adult using a different style of leadership on each occasion. In this way any personality differences between the three leaders which might have influenced the results were cancelled out.

The productivity of each group in each session was assessed by observing the boys going about their work and estimating the proportion of the total time during which they were actively working on their tasks. When overall ratings of productivity were compared, the groups were considered to have been most productive in the sessions in which they were autocratically led. The quality of the work done, however, was adjudged to have been best during the sessions under democratic leadership. An interesting further finding to emerge concerned the boys' behaviour while the leader was absent. In the course of each session the leader was called away for a brief period. In the sessions under autocratic leadership the activity level dropped sharply while the leader was out of the room, in the democratically led sessions there was no significant change in the level of activity, while in the *laissez-faire* climate productivity actually rose in the leader's absence.

This piece of research was carried out under laboratory conditions using young boys as subjects. It is not always the case that findings established in this way will hold good for the much more complex situation which obtains in later life. In this case the situation was to some extent artificial in that the boys were experiencing different styles of leadership in rapid succession from the same individual. It is doubtful, too, how far reactions of 11-year old boys provide a reliable guide to those of adult men and women who are earning their livelihood. However, since these experiments a considerable amount of further research has been carried out in the actual settings in which executive leadership takes place and much of this indicates that White and Lippitt's findings are, in fact, not irrelevant to the issues of productivity and morale in industry.

## TANNENBAUM AND SCHMIDT

One criticism of early work on leadership styles, such as that of White and Lippit and Stogdill, is that they looked at leadership styles too much in black-and-white terms. The autocratic and democratic styles or task-oriented and relationship-oriented styles which they described are extremes, whereas in practice the behaviour of many, perhaps most, leaders in business will be somewhere between the two. Among those who have made this point are Tannenbaum and Schmidt (1958), who have suggested the idea that leadership behaviour varies along a continuum and that as one moves away from the autocratic extreme the amount of subordinate participation and involvement in decision taking increases. They also suggest that the kind of leadership represented by the democratic extreme of the continuum will be rarely encountered in formal organizations.

At least four leadership styles can be located at points along such a continuum:

■ **The autocratic.** The leader takes the decisions and announces them, expecting subordinates to carry them out without question.

■ **The persuasive.** The leader at this point on the scale also takes all the decisions for the group without discussion or consultation but believes that people will be better motivated if they are persuaded that the decisions are good ones. He or she does a lot of explaining and 'selling' in order to overcome any possible resistance to what he or she wants to do. The leader also puts a lot of energy into creating enthusiasm for the goals he or she has set for the group.

■ **The consultative.** The significant feature of consultative leadership is that the leader confers with the group members *before* taking decisions and, in fact, considers their advice and their feelings when framing decisions. He or she may, of course, not always accept the subordinates' advice but they are likely to feel that they can influence the leader. Under this leadership style the decision and the full responsibility for it remain with the leader but the degree of involvement by subordinates in decision taking is very much greater than in the preceding styles.

■ **The democratic.** Using this style the leader would characteristically lay the problem before his or her subordinates and invite discussion. The leader's role is that of conference leader, or chair, rather than that of decision taker. He or she will allow the decision to emerge out of the process of group discussion, instead of imposing it on the group as its boss.

Common sense suggests there will be some situations in which each of the above styles is likely to be more appropriate than the others. In an emergency, for example, where an immediate decision is demanded, an autocratic style is likely to be most appropriate and would normally be considered justified by the group. The persuasive style would tend to fit situations in which the group leader, and he or she alone, possesses all the information on which the decision must be based and which at the same time calls for a very high level of commitment and enthusiasm on the part of group members if the task is to be carried through successfully. The consultative style is likely to be most appropriate when there is time in which to reach a considered decision and when the information on which the decision needs to be based is distributed among the members of the group. The democratic style is appropriate under similar conditions, with the important exception that this is likely to be appropriate only in those instances where the nature of the responsibility associated with the decision is such that group members are willing to share it with their leader, or alternatively the leader is willing to accept responsibility for decisions which he or she has not made personally.

The fact that different styles are appropriate to different situations would imply that the skilled leader varies his or her style according to the nature of the situation facing the group. Nevertheless, the research findings in this field indicate that individual leaders tend to employ one of the styles more consistently than the others, thus giving their overall pattern of leadership behaviour a 'flavour' which makes it possible to describe it as characteristically autocratic, persuasive, consultative or democratic.

Some work in British industry by the Research Department of Ashridge Management College was concerned with exploring employee attitudes to these four leadership styles (Sadler, 1966). People at all levels and in all fields of work in two companies were questioned, involving a total sample of over 1500. The four styles were described in a questionnaire and the employees were invited to say under which type of leader they thought they would most enjoy working. The styles were simply labelled (a), (b), (c) and (d) and the terms autocratic, persuasive, etc were not used in case they should colour the replies. The most frequently preferred style was the consultative (67 per cent), followed by the persuasive (23 per cent). The democratic style was the least preferred at 2 per cent. It is interesting that the vast majority of the respondents did, in fact, feel able to answer this question and to indicate a clear preference for one of the four.

People were also invited to state which of the four descriptions most closely corresponded to the way their own immediate managers led their sections of departments. Here a fifth response was included as an additional alternative – 'he or she does not correspond at all closely to any of them'. The results of the question on perceptions are shown in Table 5.1, in which the responses are analysed by level in the organization.

There is a tendency for the proportions who believe that they are being led in a persuasive or consultative way to fall and for the proportion regarding the boss as autocratic to rise, as one moves down the hierarchy. Among managerial level respondents, 36 per cent perceived the style of their own boss to be consultative, but this fell to 16 per cent among blue collar workers. On the other hand, only 15 per cent of managers saw their bosses as autocratic whereas 23 per cent of shopfloor workers perceived this style. The clear overall preference for the consultative style is not reflected in people's perceptions of the actual styles of their own bosses. In other words, many of the people in these two organizations who feel they would most enjoy working under consultative leadership do not believe that this is the kind of leadership they are actually experiencing.

For the sample as a whole, approximately one in four could not place their managers under one of the four leadership styles described. It is interesting to speculate on the reasons for this and on the kind of leadership pattern employed by managers whose subordinates could not fit them into one of the four categories. The next set of data throws some light on these questions.

White and Lippitt demonstrated in their laboratory experiments that different styles of leadership produced differential effects on the quantity and quality of group output. Outside the laboratory it is not easy to design studies to arrive at such neat solutions. Output is not always measurable. Where it can be measured, an additional problem is that within the whole complex structure of an industrial organization the leadership style of first-line management is only one among many important factors likely to be influencing the level of productivity. It is also the case that managers and supervisors are employed to do more than maintain the quantity and quality of output. According to the nature of the situation they may also be expected to build and maintain employee morale and to maintain discipline. Consequently, any attempts to find simple associations between work-group efficiency and leadership style are unlikely to be successful. In the Ashridge studies which took place in a marketing organization and a large research and development laboratory, it was not possible to obtain objective measures of output. It was, however, possible to compare the various perceived leadership styles of managers in terms of four criteria: subordinates' job satisfaction; subordinates' satisfaction with the company; subordinates'

**Table 5.1** *Employee perception of immediate manager's leadership style*

| | Autocratic % | Persuasive % | Consultative % | Democratic % | None of these % | No reply % |
|---|---|---|---|---|---|---|
| Managers (*n* = 126) | 15 | 30 | 36 | 6 | 12 | 2 |
| Professional/ technical (*n* = 660) | 15 | 25 | 25 | 5 | 28 | 3 |
| Salespersons (*n* = 196) | 22 | 23 | 27 | 1 | 21 | 4 |
| Supervisors (*n* = 61) | 34 | 20 | 15 | 8 | 20 | 3 |
| Clerical/secretarial (*n* = 354) | 26 | 19 | 18 | 6 | 20 | 10 |
| 'Blue-collar' workers (*n* = 113) | 23 | 16 | 16 | 5 | 36 | 4 |

confidence in immediate managers; and subordinates' ratings of their immediate manager's efficiency. The results are shown in Table 5.2.

In each case attitudes vary significantly with leadership style. The most favourable outcomes overall are associated with the consultative style, although the autocratic manager is most likely to be described as 'running things efficiently'. The least favourable responses, particularly in terms of confidence in management and the belief that the manager is running things efficiently, are associated with those managers who are not seen as falling under one of the four distinctive styles. In other words, in the light of the results shown in Table 5.2, it would appear to be very much better to have a clearly recognizable leadership style of some kind than not to have one at all.

This brings into consideration what is, in fact, a neglected aspect of the study of leadership: the question of subordinates' attitudes and expectations. Where a manager does not operate consistently in accord-ance with a recognizable style of leadership it is likely that he or she fails to provide subordinates with a clear set of expectations concerning how they should behave and what his or her reactions are likely to be as various kinds of situation arise. Other studies (for example work by Kahn, 1956), have shown that the lack of a clear set of expectations of this kind is likely to give rise to anxiety on the subordinates' part. To put this another way, although subordinates may desire a certain type of relationship with their leaders in terms, for example, of the extent to which they would like to be consulted about decisions, what they are even more in need of is a consistent relationship which enables them to know where they stand and which makes it possible for them to predict the boss's behaviour.

# CONSIDERATION AND INITIATION OF STRUCTURE

Research at the Ohio State University in the 1940s (Fleishman, 1973) using a questionnaire technique to study leadership behaviour, led to the postulation of two major dimensions of leader behaviour – *consideration* and *initiation of structure*.

Consideration is defined as behaviour evidencing concern for members of the group, such as giving recognition, nurturing self-esteem, develop-ing mutual trust, inviting participation, etc. Initiation of structure is defined as behaviours that organize the group, define relationships,

**Table 5.2** *Leadership style and subordinates' attitudes*

|  | Autocratic (n = 320) % | Persuasive (n = 352) % | Consultative (n = 367) % | Democratic (n = 379) % | None of these (n = 381) % |
|---|---|---|---|---|---|
| High job satisfaction | 72 | 81 | 84 | 81 | 66 |
| High satisfaction with organisation | 86 | 90 | 93 | 87 | 82 |
| High confidence in management | 76 | 87 | 89 | 70 | 50 |
| High rating of manager's efficiency | 38 | 30 | 35 | 27 | 12 |

specify the task and how it is to be done, emphasizing the need to hit deadlines and maintain quality, defining lines of responsibility, and clarifying roles.

This is a basic distinction to be found in a great deal of leadership research, albeit using slightly different terminology. Initiation of structure, of course, is very close to what other writers have categorized as managerial as distinct from leadership behaviour.

Several groups of researchers have studied the question of leadership styles from the starting point of the Ohio State University distinction between task-oriented behaviour and behaviour that focuses on relationships and consideration for employees. For example, in a classic series of studies, research workers at Michigan University (Katz, 1950) classified first-line supervisors under two headings: the 'production-centred supervisor' who gives greatest emphasis to task achievement; and the 'employee-centred supervisor' who gives prior attention to people's needs.

One of the studies in this series was carried out in an insurance company. The supervisors were classified as production-centred or employee-centred on the basis of their own descriptions of how they approached their jobs. At the same time groups were classified as high-producing or low-producing on the basis of production records. Out of eight supervisors classified as production-centred, only one was in charge of a group with high output. On the other hand, of nine employee-centred supervisors, six had high-producing sections.

In interpreting these findings it is possible that the supervisory style is a result rather than a cause of high productivity. In other words, it may be the case that where a section is producing good work a supervisor can afford to relax and to centre on human relations but where a group is less efficient pressure on the supervisor makes him or her become more concerned with getting results.

One weakness in these studies which was noted earlier is the somewhat artificial separation of managers into those who are employee-centred and those who are production-centred. For example, although a study in a tractor factory indicated that high-producing supervisors were those most skilled in satisfying subordinates' needs for information and support, these supervisors were no less concerned with the need to maintain high production. Kahn (1956) suggested the need to replace the employee-centred/production-centred continuum with a fourfold classification embracing two other kinds of supervisor: the one who is highly concerned both with production and the employee needs; and the one who is not very concerned with either.

# THE MANAGERIAL GRID

Among the most well-known and most influential work in the field of leadership training and development is that of Blake and Mouton who further developed the idea that each managerial leader essentially has two tasks, ie he or she must promote high morale and commitment to the job and the organization among his or her subordinates but must also ensure that the work is performed efficiently. Blake and Mouton (1964) call these aspects of the leadership role 'concern for people' and 'concern for production' respectively. They are, of course, derived from the dimensions of consideration and initiating structure identified in the Ohio State University studies referred to earlier.

They then proceed to identify five main leadership styles. This they do by measuring each type of concern on a nine-point scale, and, by placing the scales at right-angles to each other, constructing a matrix or 'grid', with 81 cells. In theory this allows for 81 different management styles combining varying degrees of 'concern for production' with varying amounts of 'concern for people'. Reading along each of the scales, the interrelationships between each type of concern can be observed, indicating variations in management style. In practice, attention is focused on five main styles as follows:

Grid score:   9.1   Maximum concern for production, minimum concern for people.

1.9   Minimum concern for production, maximum concern for people.

5.5   Halfway concern for production, halfway concern for people.

1.1   Minimum concern for production, minimum concern for people.

9.9   Maximum concern for production, maximum concern for people.

The 9.1 manager resolves conflicts between morale and efficiency by concentrating on results at the cost of morale, while the 1.9 manager concentrates on keeping people happy at the expense of results. The 5.5 manager tends to compromise; his approach is not to go all out for either better results or higher morale but to try to balance the two at a reasonably satisfactory level. The 9.9 style, however, is based on the conviction that conflicts between the demands of high performance and the needs of employees are neither necessary nor inherent and that the natural expression of human needs can lead to outstanding performance, achieving both excellent results and high morale through concentrated teamwork.

The training programmes which Blake and Mouton developed have been widely used in many countries. They are concerned with enabling people to assess their existing styles of leadership and helping them move towards the 9.9 ideal. Perhaps their most important contribution lies in popularising much of the academic research and drawing the attention of thousands of practitioners to the problem which faces all leaders, that is, how to satisfy people's needs and maintain morale while at the same time pressing for higher levels of output and greater efficiency.

# REDDIN'S 3D THEORY

An approach to leadership training similar to Blake and Mouton's managerial grid has been developed by W J Reddin (1970). This approach also takes as its starting-point the same two basic components of the leadership role, which Reddin, however, describes as 'task orientation' and 'relationships orientation'. Like Blake and Mouton, he treats these as scales and derives four basic management styles:

1.   High on task but low on relationships.

2.   High on relationships but low on task.

3.   Low on both task and relationships.

4.   High on both

However, he argues that no one of these styles is necessarily more effective than the others. Each may be equally effective depending on the situation in which it is exercised. When used effectively, the four styles are termed, respectively, *benevolent autocrat*, *developer*, *bureaucrat*, and *executive*. When used ineffectively, they become *autocrat*, *missionary*, *deserter* and *compromiser*. Reddin argues that the essential qualities of effective managerial leadership are *diagnostic skill* to evaluate the situation, and *style flexibility* to be able to select the style to fit the situation.

# RENSIS LIKERT

Rensis Likert (1961) is another highly regarded academic who carried out studies of the effectiveness of task-oriented and people-oriented leaders, this time using the terminology job-centred and employee-centred. He found that departments led by job-centred supervisors tended to be low in efficiency.

He also made a distinction between two types of autocratic leadership style: the exploitative authoritarian and the benevolent authoritarian. The former restricts communication to top-down channels, makes all key decisions without consultation and maintains considerable social distance between himself or herself and followers. The latter is more inclined to listen to followers' ideas but because followers are kept in a basically subservient position the information and ideas flowing upwards tend to be restricted to things the leader wants to hear.

# FRED FIEDLER AND CONTINGENCY THEORY

The work of Fred Fiedler (1969) has long been held in high regard by academic students of leadership, but practitioners find it difficult to come to terms with. Fiedler's starting-point was also the distinction between task-oriented leadership and consideration. He pointed out that the apparently simple question, asking which of the two approaches was most effective, had proved remarkably difficult to answer. Studies had produced evidence in favour of each point of view, leading to the hypothesis that different types of group need different types of leadership. Fiedler went beyond this, to try to establish the exact conditions under which each leadership style would be most effective.

He devised a test in which individuals were asked to think of all the people with whom he or she had ever worked and then to describe the one person with whom she or he had the greatest difficulty working – his or her least preferred co-worker (LPC). The descriptions were made in a standardised way using 20 scales with such ranges as friendly/unfriendly and co-operative/unco-operative. Each scale scored 1 to 8 with 8 indicating the favourable end of the range. Thus a person with a high LPC score is one who describes his or her least preferred co-worker in relatively favourable terms. He found that leaders with high LPC scores tended to be non-directive and considerate in their relationships with group members, while those with low LPC scores tended to be directive and task-oriented.

Fiedler then carried out studies of leadership and performance in a wide range of settings from basket ball teams to military combat groups and from shopfloor groups in industry to experimental groups in his laboratory. These studies found high correlations between the leader's LPC score and group performance. In some cases, however, the task-oriented leaders produced the best results, while in others the high performing groups were led by leaders showing consideration. He then went on to look for a way of explaining these differences and examined the influence of three variables:

▌ **The leader member relationship.** The degree to which the leader is personally accepted and liked. Fiedler argues that this is undoubtedly the most important single factor determining the interaction between a leader and the group, and suggests that it is fairly easy to lead a group in which one is liked and accepted.

▌ **Task structure.** Here Fiedler focused attention on the extent to which the task is well-defined, with verifiable outcomes. He cites as an example of a well-defined task the countdown of a space probe. The leader can prescribe each step of the operation precisely and provided people carry out their instructions correctly the task will be successfully carried out. By contrast a task such as new product development poses a very different challenge. The leader does not know what steps will lead to a satisfactory conclusion nor can he or she even indicate precisely what the end result should look like. The ill-defined task of this kind, therefore, presents a much more difficult challenge for the leader. Fiedler measured task difficulty using four variables: decision verifiability; goal clarity; goal path multiplicity; and solution specificity.

▌ **Power of position.** This was measured by a simple checklist including such items as the leader's ability to promote, and to fire and his or her rank or title.

At this point Fiedler's research design gets more complicated. Having measured each group task situation on each of these three dimensions he then identified eight possible sets of circumstances as shown in Table 5.3.

The eight sets were then arranged in order of their favourableness for the leader, assuming that leader acceptance was the most important factor, followed by task structure. Thus the most favourable situation would be an accepted and well-liked leader, a structured task and a

**Table 5.3** *Fiedler's measure of group task situation versus circumstances*

|  | Leader–member relations | Task structure | Position power |
|---|---|---|---|
| 1. | Good | Structured | Strong |
| 2. | Good | Structured | Weak |
| 3. | Good | Unstructured | Strong |
| 4. | Good | Unstructured | Weak |
| 5. | Poor | Structured | Strong |
| 6. | Poor | Structured | Weak |
| 7. | Poor | Unstructured | Strong |
| 8. | Poor | Unstructured | Weak |

leader with high position power. The next most favourable would be an accepted leader, a structured task and low position power and so on.

Fiedler then went on to check whether different situations called for different approaches on the part of the leader. This was done by relating the leader's LPC score and group performance for each of the eight types of circumstances. The results showed that directive, task-oriented leaders tended to be most effective in situations which were either very favourable or very unfavourable, while leaders oriented towards consideration were most effective in situations of intermediate difficulty.

He claimed that his results fitted well with our everyday experience. For example, when the leader is accepted and the task is clear the leader is expected to give clear instructions and the leader who is less directive under such conditions loses in esteem. We do not want an aircraft captain to ask his crew what they think he should check before take-off. At the same time, when the task is very unstructured and the leader lacks acceptance by the group it is important for the leader to take charge, otherwise the group is likely to fall apart. The non-directive leader is most effective where the task is unstructured, yet the leader is well liked. This is often the case in groups concerned with creativity.

Based on his conclusion from these studies Fiedler formulated the general proposition that the type of leadership behaviour which will be most effective is contingent on the favourableness of the task situation.

## SITUATIONAL LEADERSHIP

Hersey and Blanchard (1988) developed a particular form of contingency theory which has become well known as *situational leadership*. Making the point that the appropriateness of a leadership style is a function of the situation, they focused attention on 'subordinate maturity' as a contingent variable, by which they meant the ability and willingness of a subordinate to work without direction. Where subordinate maturity is high, a relationship-oriented style is appropriate, but where maturity is lacking a more task-oriented style will prove more effective.

## STYLE AND PERSONAL PHILOSOPHY

According to Badaracco and Ellsworth (1989), leaders resolve dilemmas in the light of their own personal philosophies. These philosophies are usually tacit rather than explicit; they involve fundamental assumptions about human nature, about the role of people in organizations, the nature of managerial work and the kinds of actions that contribute to organizational effectiveness. 'Like a geological deposit, these tacit philosophies build up over many years through the experiences and influences that shape a person's life.' They identify three such philosophies: *political* leadership, *directive* leadership and *values-driven* leadership.

▌ **Political leadership.** Leaders who work with this as their guiding philosophy may have a clear vision of their organization's future but they do not pursue their objectives head on. They keep their goals broadly defined and flexible and move incrementally, patiently and sometimes obliquely to translate the vision into reality. This approach is political in the sense of involving awareness of, and sensitivity to, the political nature of organizational life. Those who practise it may be accused of being manipulative or Machiavellian.

This philosophy is based on a set of assumptions about human behaviour in organizations. On the one hand, organizations are seen as internally divided, as a result of such forces as the interplay of self-interest, conflicts over the allocation of resources, the special-ized nature of most organizational roles and the conflicts that can arise between the goals of the company as a whole and the objectives of its various sub-units.

Another assumption is about the inherent inertia of organizations and the consequent resistance to change, preference for standard operating procedures and tendency to 'satisfice' rather than optimize.

Holding these assumptions leads to the conclusion that leaders are the captives as much as the masters of their organizations. As a result 'they must be adept at moving forward in small incremental steps and at orchestrating astutely from behind the scenes'.

▌ **Directive leadership.** This style 'involves directing a company toward clear, specific and compelling goals'. These goals are deter-mined by an objective assessment of a company's strengths and weaknesses and its competitive position. Directive leaders are clear and forceful in their relationship with followers; they confront internal conflicts; take personal responsibility for key decisions; challenge the conventional wisdom; and place a great deal of reliance on structure and systems for control and decision making.

Such leaders share three assumptions. First, they believe that people are motivated more by internal forces than by external stimuli. They motivate people by offering them stretching and challenging goals and the potential for pride in what they can achieve. Second, they see it as a major task for the leader to create cohesion in the organization as a whole and to prevail over the tendency for frag-mentation and internal divisions. Third, they prefer substance to style and action to reaction. Jack Welch of GE is cited as the most well-known exponent of this style.

▌ **Values-driven leadership.** This philosophy is not just an alternative to the other two but one which both enhances and transcends them. It acknowledges the political nature of organizational life and the need for direction and focus on substance. It holds, however, that a leader's behaviour must also serve purposes and reflect values with which followers can identify. The main task of the leader is seen as the process of energizing followers to value actions which support overall corporate purposes rather than their own self-interest.

Badaracco and Ellsworth relate this approach to James McGregor Burns' concept of transforming leadership. As examples of values-driven leaders, they cite Dave Packard of Hewlett Packard, Thomas Watson Jr of IBM and James Burke of Johnson & Johnson.

# TWO CONTRASTING LEADERSHIP STYLES

Pascale (1990) gives a detailed account of the leadership style of two prominent business leaders – Jack Welch of GE and Donald Petersen of Ford.

On his way to the top in GE, Jack Welch built a highly successful $2 billion business in plastics and subsequently turned around the company's ailing medical diagnostics business. Later, as vice chairman, he began transforming GE Capital into a major financial services company.

On taking charge of GE as a whole, Welch initially focused on improving earnings. He moved aggressively to prune out weak businesses and cut costs. Between 1981 and 1986, he eliminated 130,000 jobs, or 25 per cent of the workforce. Not surprisingly these actions created an atmosphere of insecurity and mistrust. In Welch's words, 'I didn't start with a morale problem, I created it!'

In the absence of any sense of crisis, Welch believed that he had to act in such a way that the company would be shocked out of its complacency. He became known as 'Neutron Jack' (a reference to the neutron bomb which destroys people but leaves buildings standing). *Fortune* magazine listed him as one of America's 10 toughest bosses. There is no doubt that however ruthless Welch's actions appeared, they called for great courage and the willingness to attract and absorb immense hostility and criticism.

From 1986 on Welch concentrated on building the business, having developed a strategy based on focusing on those business areas in which GE already had a number one or strong number two position. He grouped GE's portfolio into three areas – core, services and high technology – and designated businesses outside these as candidates for divestment. He made some major acquisitions to strengthen GE in its chosen markets, including RCA and the Employee Reinsurance Company. He regarded his task at this stage as fixing the 'hardware'. From 1987 he turned his attention to the 'software', achieving productivity growth through the bottom-up initiatives of employees. He began spending a considerable part of his time in meetings with employees at all levels, delivering four messages consistently:

▌ Be number one or a strong number two in your business or get out.

▌ Do not finesse the numbers. Tell it as it is and face the harsh realities of your situation.

■   Go for excellence in everything we do.

■   Take risks – a well-reasoned failure will not be punished.

Welch believed that the role of the leader was to create a vision, articulate it, own it passionately and drive its implementation. He believed,
too, in openness – 'tell people the truth, because they know the truth
anyway'. Like many charismatic leaders, he ignored the formal channels
of communication. Despite his efforts at exhortation, progress initially
was slow. The gap between Welch's vision and the reality of organizational life in the divisions remained large.

During the next phase of his work, from 1987 on, Welch set about
simplifying GE's complex organization structure and streamlining its
processes. Layers of management were removed. Business review
reports were reduced from pages of figures and detail to one page of
prose. Corporate staff was cut back sharply. He initiated a process known
as 'work-out', which was aimed at winkling out and removing thousands
of bad working habits that had accumulated at GE over the years.

Reaction to Welch's leadership style, according to Pascale varied
depending on how close people were to him. For those who got to know
him personally, his aggressive, 'steamroller' style was more than balanced
by qualities such as courage, sincerity and his dedication to GE's success.
From a greater distance, he seemed overbearing and instrumental in the
way he dealt with people.

Welch, of course, was well aware of the extent of criticism of his
approach. One of his responses was to commission a project that would
involve thousands of people in developing a GE statement of values. The
result was a set of five 'business characteristics' and six 'industrial' ones.
The business was to be lean, agile and creative. Employees were to feel
ownership of it and rewards were to be commensurate with risk and
performance. Individuals were to face reality, to exercise leadership, to
be open with each other, to keep things simple, to have integrity and to
show respect for each other. The Welch stamp on these is unmistakable.

In order to drive them home they were incorporated into the performance evaluation system. Pascale observes, 'we catch the paradox of
his iron-willed, top-down approach grappling with a phenomenon that
has to be internalised voluntarily. He does talk about and believe in GE's
values – such as empowerment – but his propensity to muscle implementation through is also evident'.

In an epilogue to his autobiography (Welch, 2001) he reflects on his
achievements:

We took a bureaucracy and we shook it. We created a world class organisation, whose excellence is accepted on every continent. I believe the GE
I'm leaving is a true meritocracy, a place filled with excited people, with
good values and high integrity. It's a company that lives for great ideas,
relishes change. Great people, not great strategies made it work. We spent
extraordinary time recruiting, training, developing and rewarding the
best. Our reach and our success would have been limited without the best
people stretching to become better.

Pascale contrasts Welch's style with the highly effective but clearly not
charismatic leadership style of Donald Petersen of the Ford Motor
Company. At the beginning of the 1980s Ford was in serious trouble,
having made the huge loss of $2.2 billion. Petersen brought two key
qualities to bear on this disastrous situation. First, he was a 'product
man', in that most of his career had been spent in the design and manufacturing functions. Secondly, he had a vision of how Ford could begin
to mobilize the talents and energy of its workforce.

An engineering graduate, Petersen served in the US marines during
the Second World War and obtained his MBA at Stamford. He started at
Ford as a product planner, working on the development of the Thunder-
bird model in the 1950s and on the Mustang in the 1960s. In the late
1970s, he was appointed to lead Ford's International Automotive Oper-
ations Division.

In his early years at Ford he had seen at first hand the dysfunctional
effects of 'turf wars' between functions and how quality had been
accorded lower priority than cost accounting and financial controls.
Along with a lot of fellow Ford employees, he wanted to see the company
restored to pride of place in the automobile industry.

Under Petersen's leadership, Ford did in fact achieve a remarkable
turnaround. From a total loss of $3 billion over the period 1980–1982,
it recovered to achieve, by 1986, greater profits than GM for the first
time since 1924 and, by 1987, to break all previous industry records for
profitability, as well as ranking number three in quality among all US
companies. The Taurus model won the 'Triple Crown' in 1987 – being
selected Car of the Year, Best Domestic Car and Top Car. Pascale poses
the question, 'How, then, does an individual such as Don Petersen –
reticent and unassuming – execute such a daring turn around of such
magnitude?'

Petersen explains the fact that Henry Ford II chose him to be president
of the company simply because he was the only member of top management with strong product development experience at a time when the

company desperately needed successful new products. 'My dreams about how this company could be different organisationally played no role in my getting the president's job.' Described by one observer as 'the opposite of Henry Ford II, Lee Iacocca and a host of other egotistical and dominating managers who have played significant leadership roles at Ford', Petersen was a leader who lived and breathed participative management and subordinated his ego to the needs of the business.

Pascale's answer to his own question is that Petersen succeeded because through persistence and personal example he opened up the Ford hierarchy to the ideas and initiative of those at lower levels. In a word, he succeeded through his ability to make involvement not just a word but a living reality. One of his first actions was to call an off-site meeting for his six direct reports. On the agenda was 'How are we going to work together as a group to help address the problems facing Ford?' Pascale records that on this occasion and others, Petersen exercised superb skill as a group facilitator, having considerable intuition and empathy, and the ability to ask penetrating questions. He transferred the strongly bureaucratic Policy and Strategy Committee into an effective informal breakfast get-together where 'we can talk to one another in shirt sleeves'.

In Pascale's view, Ford is the only large business to have truly transformed itself. Petersen, undoubtedly the main agent of this change, is the supreme example of the leader as 'catalyst'. Self-effacing, quiet, definitely not charismatic, his example challenges the validity of the idea of the leader as hero. Pascale recalls an occasion in 1989 when Petersen addressed the MBA class at the Harvard Business School. Petersen, he says, was ill at ease on the platform, quiet and self-effacing, and the students were left wondering how he could have carried out such a remarkable transformation. The answer is that he did not personally 'carry it out'. Through his involving style he enabled large numbers of employees at all levels to do so.

# SUMMARY

The various theories and studies of leadership styles can now be drawn together and summed up in the following propositions which provide useful guidance for practising managers:

1.  Leadership in management involves concern both for task performance and for people's needs, aspirations and expectations.

2.  Concern for people requires paying attention to, and knowledge of, the influences which motivate people as members of groups and as individuals.

3.  The way in which a manager chooses to exercise leadership (his or her leadership style) can have a strong influence on the performance, motivation and morale of his or her subordinates.

4.  There is no single style likely to be effective in all circumstances. The effectiveness of management style will vary according to the situation. This includes the general cultural setting in which leadership takes place and the extent to which the values of society are ones which favour autocratic or democratic forms of social control. Western societies are characterized generally by movement away from autocratically controlled social institutions and towards ones which are democratically constituted. This trend has inevitable implications for people's attitudes to the legitimacy of leadership and authority in the work situation. Increasingly, autocratic styles of leadership are being challenged not only in terms of their effectiveness but on moral grounds.

5.  In consequence, managers should be prepared to be flexible and adjust style to circumstances. They should, however, avoid seeming to be inconsistent; if they adopt a different style in a particular set of circumstances the reasons for the change in style should be made clear to subordinates.

# 6

# Recruiting and selecting future leaders

Organizations, if they are to survive, need a continuing supply of persons capable of and motivated to exercise leadership. There are two distinct approaches to securing an adequate supply of leaders. One is to recruit directly into senior positions from outside the organization people with a good track record as leaders. The other is for an organization to 'grow its own timber' and thus ensure an adequate flow into leadership roles of people who were originally recruited as graduates or school leavers. Most organizations pursue both approaches, usually with a bias one way or the other. Those which fill a significant number of senior positions from within share the many difficult problems associated with the identification of their so-called 'high-flyers': These problems include the following:

- First there is the confusion between management and leadership to be resolved. Is the organization clear about what it wants: managers, leaders or a combination of the two?

- Given that people who are currently in their twenties are unlikely in most instances to reach senior positions in large organizations until their mid-thirties or later, there is a requirement to make a judgement about future business conditions and their implications for the nature of the leadership role in the future.

- Given that there is reasonable confidence in such judgements, further judgements are needed in order to determine the qualities and skills that will be needed on the part of those who will fill such future roles.

▌ Given that the qualities and skills which will be required have been reasonably well identified, there is a further requirement to identify which young people have the greatest potential for developing these qualities and attributes.

## THE FUTURE CONTEXT OF ORGANIZATIONS

The only certain thing about the future is that it will be different from the present. Given the current rapid pace of change, it is likely to be very different. This being so it is likely that different leadership skills will be needed in the future, so the difficult task of trying to forecast the key changes which will have taken place in 10 or 15 years' time cannot be avoided. At the same time its extreme difficulty cannot be overestimated. As Drucker (1969) pointed out in his brilliant study of the business environment in the late 1960s we cannot predict the future simply by extrapolation from the past. The natural tendency when forecasting is to be aware of current issues of critical importance and to see them as trends stretching ever onwards into the future. Yet, as Drucker pointed out, the most significant changes in terms of their consequences for business organizations are more likely to arise from discontinuities than from well-established trends. Events of global importance such as the sudden disintegration of the Soviet bloc are inherently unpredictable. Given this, any scenarios of the future must be provisional and tentative and will need constant revision as time unfolds the reality of events.

There have been many books written about the future of the business environment as we move into the early years of the 21st century. Distilling from them a common list of anticipated changes results in the following set of factors.

▌ Continuation of rapid change generally.

▌ Continuation of underlying rates of economic growth.

▌ Intensification of competition.

▌ Increasing globalization of business.

▌ Continuation of rising customer expectations in respect of product and service quality.

▌ Continuation of rising expectations on the part of employees in respect of the quality of working life.

I Further considerable progress in the field of information technology.

I Considerable strides in the field of biotechnology.

I Increasing public concern about the impact of economic activity on such things as personal health and safety and the environment.

I Successful avoidance of major international conflicts.

'Surprises' which might upset this conventional view are by definition subject only to speculation but might include such events as the discovery of extremely cheap renewable energy via nuclear fusion or the breaking up of the European Community.

Taking the conventional view, however, the implications for the organizational context of management in the future are held to be the following:

I Organizations will need to become more fast-moving, less bureaucratic, more responsive to external forces, more proactive in seeking change.

I Organizations will, on the one hand, become more decentralised or fragmented but will, on the other hand, be integrated through a common culture and information technology based networks.

I Organizations will need to improve their capacity to innovate.

I Decision-making processes will take place increasingly across organizations in line with processes rather than vertically in the context of traditional functional hierarchies.

I Organizations will become increasingly dependent on the quality of their human resource management for the achievement of competitive advantage.

I Organizations will increasingly include members from many different cultural backgrounds.

I Pressures for environmentally friendly processes and products will intensify.

I Similarly, pressures for socially responsible policies and transparent reporting will increase.

# THE FUTURE ROLE OF BUSINESS LEADERSHIP

These changes in turn point to some key features of the leadership role in the future, particularly at senior level:

▌ More emphasis on creating and sharing a vision of the future in an uncertain world, on creating an awareness of the need for change and successfully leading the implementation of it.

▌ Greater sensitivity to and understanding of the business environment.

▌ Greater involvement in lateral, non-hierarchical relationships and transactions including collaborative relationships with customers, suppliers and joint venture partners.

▌ More involvement in community relations and with pressure groups.

# THE FUTURE LEADER

What kinds of persons will be required to fill such roles? Organizations tend to look for the answers to questions of this kind in two different ways. One approach is to try to specify the personal qualities that will be required; things such as intelligence, personality traits, particular aptitudes, etc. The other is to focus more on the skills and knowledge that need to be acquired. Somewhat confusingly, the term competencies is sometimes used to cover both aspects.

As an example of the personal qualities approach one of the companies studied in the Ashridge research project *Management for the Future* (Ashridge Management College, 1988) listed the qualities required as:

▌ Independence.

▌ Openness to change.

▌ Assertiveness.

▌ Being respected.

▌ Being a good motivator.

▌ Having drive.

▌ Loyalty.

▌ Having tact.

In another study (Sadler, 1993) a French company specified 'people who are creative, adaptable, ambitious for themselves, who are courageous and assertive, open-minded people who think in an international way'.

Although these lists, like other similar ones, are put forward as describing future leaders, they could as well be describing today's leaders or even yesterday's leaders. As we saw in an earlier chapter a very wide range of qualities has been identified as linked to success as a leader. Even allowing for valid distinctions between one organizational culture and another, however, the lack of consensus among such lists is disconcerting. If, however, it is accepted that such lists of qualities have more than face validity, the issue remains of how these qualities are to be validly measured or assessed.

# SELECTION AND ASSESSMENT METHODS

Among the range of techniques in use, the following are the most common.

## Appraisals of potential

Conducted by the assessment of listed personal qualities or competencies:

▌ by superiors;

▌ by peers (rarely);

▌ by subordinates (even more rarely);

▌ by all three groups.

Three-hundred-and-sixty degree feedback is growing in popularity. The use of 360° feedback instruments was perhaps the most significant management innovation in the 1990s. Its use is widespread, and increasing. A review of the academic and business press indicates that over 65 per cent of large US companies, including the likes of Motorola and AMOCO, acknowledge their use of multi-rater assessment, particularly for middle and upper management. In Europe, a wide variety of either tailored or commercially available tools are in use by an increasing number of companies. This means that thousands, perhaps millions, of individuals have received feedback on their work performance from individuals in their work groups.

The competencies required in the future leaders are normally derived from today's senior managers by means of interviews or questionnaires. A typical approach for a large company is that of Philips. Once a year the divisional vice-presidents meet with representatives of the human resources function to review succession planning in general and the pool of young people of high potential in particular. They employ a corporate potential appraisal system which identifies a number of personality characteristics which by experience have been shown to be predictive of future career success. In this case validation studies have been carried out by a qualified psychologist and are updated from time to time to take account of changed circumstances including changing views as to what constitutes effective managerial leadership behaviour.

## Psychometric tests

The use of various kinds of personality tests in industry has been increasing sharply in recent years alongside the growing interest in leadership. The trend has not been without its critics. Blinkhorn and Johnson (1991), for example, examined a number of validation studies and found that the majority were statistically flawed: they concluded that there were no grounds for supposing that personality tests predict performance at work to any useful extent. Although they did not look specifically at attempts to predict performance in leadership their results suggest the need for caution in relying overmuch on test results.

Defenders of the tests (who are not necessarily free from bias) deploy several arguments in their favour. Six UK chartered psychologists presented their views in an article in *Personnel Management* (Crabb, 1992), making a number of points including the following:

▌ Validity coefficients, while not large compared with those obtained in intelligence tests, are nevertheless large enough to be useful.

▌ Tests are most useful when interpreted by qualified and experienced psychologists who understand the personality theories on which they are based.

▌ Tests are seldom used in isolation from other selection methods.

The tests fall into two broad categories according to the psychological theories of personality on which they are based. One approach follows the theories of Carl Jung. The most well known test in this area is the Myers Briggs Type Inventory, which has been in use since the 1920s and is widely used in industry today. This provides a measure or indicator of personality by examining eight behavioural preferences which are grouped into four scales. The preferences from each scale are combined so as to identify 16 personality types. The four scales are as follows:

▌ **Extroversion or introversion (E or I).** Those at the extroversion end of this continuum are energized by the external world of people, events and activities, while those at the introversion extreme prefer the internal world of ideas, emotions and thought processes.

▌ **Sensing or intuition (S or N).** This is about how people prefer to handle information. Sensing involves a preference for concrete reality and for taking in information through the five senses. Those who prefer an intuitive approach look to a sixth sense for ideas; they like to imagine what might be rather than focus on what already exists.

▌ **Thinking or feeling (T or F).** Thinking involves making decisions on the basis of logical thought and using reason, while feeling types reach decisions based more on values and feelings.

▌ **Judging or perceiving (J or P).** A preference for judging is a preference for living life in a planned and organized way, while a preference for perceiving reflects a desire for a more spontaneous and flexible life and the ability to tolerate uncertainty.

Hirsh and Kummerow (1987) set out the different approaches to leadership associated with each of the 16 types. The type which constituted the largest single group in a sample of 1000 managers attending programmes at Ashridge Management College is ISTJ. ISTJ types are described as thorough, painstaking, systematic, hard working and careful with detail. Their approach to leadership involves using experience and knowledge of the facts to make decisions, building on reliable and consistent performance as the basis for taking charge, respecting traditional, hierarchical authority, rewarding those who follow the rules and paying attention to immediate and practical organizational needs. This is scarcely the approach best suited to the demands of the organization of the future and it is certainly unlikely to be inspirational. ENTJ types are described as logical, organized, structured, objective and decisive. Their approach to leadership is to take an action-oriented energetic approach. They provide a long-range vision for the organization, they are direct and can be tough when necessary, they enjoy tackling complex problems, but can appear impatient and domineering. This would seem to be an accurate portrait of Jack Welch, former chief executive of General Electric. Tomorrow's leaders may need to be more like the ENFJ type: interpersonally skilled, understanding, tolerant, appreciative and facilitators of good communication. Their approach to leadership involves leading through personal enthusiasm, using a participative approach, being responsive to followers' needs, challenging the organization to match its actions to its values and inspiring change.

An alternative approach to personality measurement favours the conceptualization of personality in terms of discrete traits. The most well-known test of this kind is Cattell's 16-factor personality inventory, which compares people in terms of 16 traits each of which represents a dimension or facet of the total personality. Traits particularly relevant to leadership qualities include the range from being group dependent and a follower to being self-sufficient and resourceful and the range from being apprehensive, self-reproaching and worrying to being self assured, serene and confident.

Another test frequently used when selecting leaders is the FIRO-B. The letters stand for Fundamental Interpersonal Relations Orientation-Behaviour. Two aspects are measured: expressed social behaviour (e); and wanted behaviour in others (w). These behaviours have three dimensions: inclusion, control and affection. This test is helpful in providing insights into how an individual relates to others in a group situation.

The Kirton Adaptation/Innovation Inventory is another test frequently used to assess leadership potential. It is based on the observation that some people tended to make incremental changes to existing situations, while others prefer to change the system as a means of achieving improvements.

## Questionnaire inventories

The most well-known instrument of this type is the Leader Behaviour Questionnaire (LBQ) developed at Columbia University. This has 50 items grouped into 10 scales, measuring the following dimensions of leadership:

■ Focus.

■ Trustworthiness.

■ Communication skill.

■ Respect for others.

■ Acceptance of risk.

■ Bottom line orientation.

■ Positive use of power.

■ Long-term orientation.

■ Organizational leadership.

■ Cultural leadership.

The instrument was used in a study of 60 high school principals where it was found that the schools of those principals who behaved like leaders significantly outperformed the others.

## Assessment centres

These involve various group exercises and individual tasks as well as psychometrics and interviews. They grew out of the selection methods used by military organizations to select officers, beginning with experiments in the German army before the Second World War. The techniques were subsequently developed by the British Army War Office Selection Boards and by the US Office of Strategic Services. After the war their adoption in industry spread slowly, led by America's AT&T.

All of these have a degree of face validity but given the inherent difficulty of validation research and the period of time likely to elapse between the assessment of an individual's personal qualities and his or her appointment to the board of directors (assuming the individual stays with the organization for that period of time) there is little serious validation research by companies.

# CHARACTERISTICS OF THOSE WHO MAKE IT TO THE TOP

One approach has been to study the attributes of current business leaders and use them as a guide to the prediction of future performance. This method suffers from the obvious drawback that it is based on factors associated with success in the past and if there is to be significant change in the nature of leadership in the future these factors may have little relevance or may even be counter-indicative.

A study of 45 UK chief executives – people who had made it to the top – by Cox and Cooper (1988) using the Cattell 16-factor personality test, found that the scores of the sample were widely distributed over most scales, pointing to the conclusion that no one personality profile can be said to be typical of the successful chief executive. However, 26 of the executives took the Kirton Adaptation/Innovation Inventory test. All scored in the top half of the distribution, indicating they were innovators rather than adapters, and 54 per cent came into the top 20 per cent for the population as a whole, indicating that they are strong innovators.

In addition, 30 took a Type A/Type B test, developed by R W Borne. The concept of A and B types was originally developed by Rosenman and his colleagues during a study of patients with coronary heart disease. Type A people are competitive, high-achieving, aggressive, hasty, impatient and restless. They have explosive speech patterns, tenseness of facial muscles and appear to be under pressure. They are so deeply involved in their work as to neglect other aspects of their lives. The results of the 30 CEOs were highly significant: 57 per cent were type A1, of which there are only 10 per cent in the population at large.

Cox and Cooper also reviewed several other similar studies from both sides of the Atlantic. The overall conclusions to be drawn from these various pieces of research indicated that high-flyers tended to share the following characteristics:

▍ Determination.

▍ Ability to learn from adversity.

▍ Capable of grasping chances when presented.

▍ Strong achievement drive.

▍ Strong self-control.

▌ A well-integrated set of values among which integrity, independence, initiative, people and relationships feature strongly.

▌ Moderate risk taking.

▌ Clear personal and organizational objectives.

▌ High dedication to the job.

▌ Motivated by the work itself rather than by external rewards.

▌ A well-organized life.

▌ A pragmatic as distinct from intellectual approach to problem solving.

▌ A high level of 'people skills'.

▌ A high level of innovative ability.

## THE SKILLS AND KNOWLEDGE AND EXPERIENCE APPROACH

This approach, too, is exemplified from the Ashridge research quoted previously and which offers the following profile of the skills tomorrow's business leader will need:

▌ Awareness of and ability to relate to the economic, social and political environment.

▌ Ability to lead in a turbulent environment.

▌ Ability to do so within complex organization structures.

▌ Capacity to be innovative and to initiate change.

▌ Ability to lead people with widely differing and changing values and expectations.

Two questions are raised by such lists. First, are these skills really different from those needed by today's top people? (Given that they result from 'surprise free' forecasts it is not perhaps surprising if they are not that different.) Second, as with the personal qualities, how are we to assess the extent to which young managers have the potential to develop such skills?

# THE BACKGROUNDS OF BRITISH CEOS

Research carried out by Norburn (1989) set out to determine whether CEOs of large British companies demonstrated different characteristics from other members of top management. Three hypotheses were set up as follows:

▌ CEOs will demonstrate significantly different corporate experiences from those experienced by others.

▌ CEOs will demonstrate significantly different perceptions of self, of their own beliefs and attitudes.

▌ CEOs will have experienced significantly different domestic and educational influences.

The corporate experiences taken into account included such variables as length of tenure with current company, number of previous employers, experience of different functions and experience of running own business.

The self-perception factors included aspiration level, self-perception of management style, drinking, smoking, exercise, sleep, response to stress and importance of family life and religion. The domestic influences included educational attainment, achievement at sports, childhood experiences, siblings, birth position, marital status, number of children and outside interests.

The sample consisted of 450 of Britain's 500 largest companies as listed in *The Times 500*. The CEOs in the sample were sent a personal letter requesting their participation in the research, along with three other members of top management. A response rate of 24 per cent was achieved. The results can be summarized as follows:

▌ **Corporate experience factors.** Of the variables, nine showed a significant difference at the 0.05 level and one at the 0.10 level. CEOs had longer tenure with current company and had worked for fewer companies. They had more multi-functional experience and were more likely to have worked overseas. They were more likely to have run their own companies. They worked longer hours and were more likely to spend nights away from home.

▌ **Self-perception.** Only seven out of 22 variables discriminated. These were: an avowed intention to stay on the job despite becoming financially independent; the assertion that they would take up the same career again, given the chance; they were more likely to have considered running their own business; felt it best to stay with one company; had experienced patronage during their career; and were less likely than other members of top management to perceive their management style as participative.

▌ **Domestic factors.** Under this heading also seven factors (out of 20) discriminated. These were having attended university; having only a first degree (mainly in the Arts); having had a childhood upbringing outside the UK; they had more children; and were more likely to be divorced. It is interesting that characteristics identified in other studies, particularly having had single parents and birth order failed to discriminate.

Norburn concluded that his results demonstrated that British CEOs are, indeed, 'a breed apart'! Of 59 variables tested, 42 per cent discriminated. The strongest influences were to do with corporate factors and the weakest were factors associated with education, upbringing and domestic circumstances. The major unifying and underlying set of influences emerged as one of exposure to a wide range of influences: in childhood, the experience of either an urban, cosmopolitan or colonial culture; the stimulus of an Arts degree; rapid early exposure to a range of business functions, followed by international experience and profit responsibility.

## SELECTION PITFALLS

Given the very real difficulties associated with the process of validly identifying high flyers, it is not surprising that there are serious doubts about the whole process. Two potential pitfalls are commonly stressed. The first is the natural tendency for senior managers, when assessing leadership potential and selecting 'high-flyers', to choose people in their own image and people who seem to fit in well, thus perpetuating the existing organizational culture rather than preparing it for radical change.

The second pitfall is the self-fulfilling prophecy. If the young managers who are initially chosen to be part of the accelerated development programme for high-flyers are then given early responsibility and other development opportunities, they will more or less automatically rise up through the hierarchy providing they do not actually commit any disastrous errors while their erstwhile colleagues, deprived of such opportunities, never get the chance to show what, given similar developmental treatment, they might have achieved.

# SUMMARY

Selecting tomorrow's leaders is a vitally important yet very difficult task. It involves making judgements about the ways in which organizations in the future might be different from today's organizations and about the kinds of leadership behaviour that will be needed in the future.

There is then the equally difficult task of trying to identify which of today's young recruits have the greatest potential to develop into tomorrow's successful leaders.

There is a fair degree of consensus as to the ways in which organizations will change, reflecting three main influences:

▌  the impact of developments in information technology;

▌  the increasing intensity of global competition;

▌  increasing public concern about the impact of economic activity on the environment and on living standards in the developing countries.

Organizations will need to change in the following ways:

▌  become less bureaucratic and hierarchical, and more proactive in seeking change;

▌  become more decentralized, relying more and more on sophisticated IT systems for integration;

▌  become more innovative;

▌  become more culturally diverse in membership;

▌  become more dependent on highly talented employees; and

▌  become more aware of the need to be environmentally and socially responsible.

In consequence, leaders will need to focus more on:

▌  creating and sharing a vision of the organization's future and successfully implementing change;

■ extending their influence via lateral, non-hierarchical relationships, both internally and externally;

■ developing a sensitivity to and involvement with various stakeholder groups in the environment.

Selecting future leaders will call for the deployment of a wide range of methods, including:

■ assessments of potential by peers and subordinates, as well as by superiors;

■ psychometric profiling;

■ leadership skills inventories;

■ assessment centres that combine a range of techniques;

■ studies of the qualities of those who have already made it to the top.

Two main dangers in this process are:

■ By taking today's most effective leaders as role models, perpetuating today's patterns of leadership behaviour into a future in which they become increasingly inappropriate.

■ The 'crown prince' syndrome: if those initially selected as 'high flyers' are given early responsibility and are supported by intensive development processes, then their eventual arrival at the top becomes a form of self-fulfilling prophecy.

# 7

# The development process

The fundamental challenge facing business in the 21st century will be meeting the needs of consumers and shareholders. . . in a way that balances economic, environmental and social requirements. . . The task for business schools is to engage young leaders and give them a long-term vision of success that includes social responsibility. Companies must behave differently in the next century, and will require new leadership. (Bill Ford)

## CAN LEADERSHIP BE TAUGHT?

Handy (1992) puts it this way: leadership skills cannot be taught 'but they can be learnt or, rather, discovered, fostered and allowed to grow'. For leadership to develop, he asserts, the following four things are necessary. First, there must be room to manoeuvre, the opportunity to change things, exercise initiative, experiment and make mistakes. Second, the leader must believe in himself or herself. Self-confidence is frequently rooted in a strong sense of purpose or mission, as in the case of Margaret Thatcher. Third, the leader should have a very broad perspective and not be blinkered as a result of a very narrow range of experience. Finally, an important factor is a capacity to tolerate loneliness. Leaders may be respected and trusted but will not necessarily be loved. 'Wise leaders take time to be by themselves' and understand the need for opportunities to reflect.

According to Bennis and Nanus (1985), leadership is something that can be learned by anyone, taught to everyone, and denied to no one. In life, only a few will lead nations, but more will lead companies. Even more will lead departments or small groups. Those who aren't department heads will probably be supervisors. Like other complex skills, some people start out with more fully formed leadership abilities than others. But the relevant skills can be learned, developed, and improved upon.

It is important to distinguish between leadership development programmes and leadership training courses. A course, as the term implies, is a single event that may last anything from a day to several weeks, the purpose of which is to improve the effectiveness in leadership of those attending. A leadership development programme, however, is a series of related events, including courses but also such things as mentoring and coaching, job assignments, attendance at an assessment/development centre, learning sets and/or various forms of feedback.

In a previous chapter a clear distinction was drawn between two processes: leadership and management. When looking at current practice it is apparent that this distinction is not always made. Some so-called leadership development courses are really about developing managerial skills; some management development programmes include modules on leadership.

In the majority of cases, where leadership development programmes exist, involvement in them is confined to so-called 'high flyers' – young men and women, usually graduates, who are identified as having the potential to attain senior management positions in a hierarchical structure. In only a minority of cases is this kind of development opportunity open to others such as knowledge professionals or technicians, let alone front-line employees in production or customer service. (One exception to this is the use by companies of outdoor training courses involving an activity such as abseiling, orienteering, canoeing or sailing, where young people drawn from the shop floor or its equivalent are frequently nominated. In most cases, however, such courses are isolated events and not part of a structured development programme.)

A key element in any leadership development programme is the opportunities for learning offered by job assignments. The early assumption of real responsibility is seen as providing particularly useful experience from which many lessons may be learned, subject to appropriate feedback and coaching.

Kotter (1988) identifies the following developmental practices:

▌ Assessment/development centres.

▌ Career planning discussions with bosses.

▌ Developmental job opportunities.

▌ Availability of information on job opportunities.

▌ Special programmes for those with leadership potential.

▌ External development programmes.

▌ Strategic management processes designed to clarify what the business will be like five to ten years ahead and how many/what kind of leadership roles will be needed.

▌ The rewarding of managers for developing the leadership skills of their own subordinates.

▌ Helping people to develop the capacity to manage their own development.

▌ Mentoring and/or coaching.

▌ The use of feedback.

▌ Adding additional responsibilities to current jobs.

Mentoring and coaching are being increasingly used as developmental processes. Obviously the effectiveness of mentoring critically depends on the suitability of the mentor as a role model for a future senior manager and on his or her competence in the mentoring role. Where mentors are drawn from the ranks of existing top managers there is a danger of perpetuating role models that are inappropriate for tomorrow's world.

# THE RESEARCH FINDINGS

Research findings on this subject have been summarized by McCauley (1986) of the US Center for Creative Leadership. Despite the fact that she writes from the perspective of an institution devoted to research and education in leadership she fails to clarify the distinction between the development of managerial ability and the development of leadership. She has grouped the material under the headings of job assignments; other people and relationships; hardships; and training.

## Job assignments

On-the-job experience, particularly when it involves the early assumption of real responsibility, is seen as providing the most useful learning opportunities. McCauley quotes AT&T's Management Progress Study which tracked a group of managers over a 20-year period. Initially the sample consisted of 422 who went through a three-and-a-half-day assessment centre. At the end of the assessment process the assessors made predictions as to which would progress to at least middle management level.

Overall there was a significant correlation between the predictions and the level achieved. However, among the college graduates who were predicted to fail but who subsequently experienced challenging job assignments, 61 per cent actually reached top management. Of those who were predicted to succeed but who subsequently did not have challenging jobs, only 30 per cent made it as far as middle management.

Those concerned with ensuring a new generation of leadership for the organization should focus on three factors, argues Morgan McCall (1998). Drawing on a range of research and case studies, McCall contends that the most important single factor in executive development is exposure to the right kinds of growth experiences and that the right kinds of growth experiences greatly depend on the company's values and strategy. Leadership development involves exposing those individuals who can learn most from such experiences to a diverse blend of them.

By implication:

▪ Those who are most qualified for an open position may learn the least from it, and therefore recruitment should reach more widely.

▪ Focus not just on jobs that are most important for the business, but also on jobs that provide the richest and most productive developmental experiences for those who will eventually lead the business.

▪ Reward managers not only for achieving the best results but also for cultivating the best creators of future results.

The 'basic principle is simple,' says McCall, 'people learn most by doing things they haven't done before.' If fresh experience is the finest instructor, identification of what's new becomes critical.

A research group at the Center for Creative Leadership (McCall, Lombardo and Morrison, 1988) concluded that five or more of the following challenges needed to be present in assignments:

▮ Success and failure should both be possible and evident to others.

▮ The situation should involve the leader being left alone to cope without access to higher authority.

▮ It should involve working with new people or unusually large numbers of people or people known to be difficult.

▮ Working under unusually severe pressure, eg very tight deadlines or very substantial cost at risk.

▮ Having to influence people over whom the leader has no authority.

▮ Coping with change, uncertainty or ambiguity.

▮ Performing while being closely watched by people who have the power to influence future career prospects.

▮ Exercising team leadership in stretching circumstances.

▮ Handling a task with major strategic implications or which is intellectually stretching.

▮ Working with a particularly effective or ineffective boss.

▮ Dealing with a situation in which some key factor is missing, eg adequate resources or vital knowledge.

The researchers suggest no less than 88 specific developmental assignments. These are divided into five groups as follows:

▮ Small projects and start-ups which mainly emphasize persuasion, learning new things quickly, working under time pressure and with new people.

▮ Small scope 'jumps' in responsibility which emphasize team-building, individual responsibility, dealing with the boss and time pressures.

▮ Small strategic assignments which emphasize intellectual demands and influencing skills.

▮ Course work and coaching assignments which reveal gaps in one's own knowledge or skill.

▮ Activities away from work which emphasize individual leadership and working with new people.

Kotter (1988) selects the following career experiences as being of crucial importance in the development of leadership skills.

■ Significant challenge early on. People who are given opportunities to lead and to accept responsibility at a relatively early age learn from their failures and setbacks as well as from their successes.

■ Opportunities at a later career stage to broaden out through such experiences as a lateral move to a different function, attendance on a lengthy general management course, secondment to a voluntary organization or assignment to a special project team.

■ A decentralised organization structure which pushes responsibility down to lower levels. Johnson & Johnson, 3M, Hewlett Packard and General Electric are quoted by Kotter as prime examples. In Europe ABB has a similar structure.

■ Processes which ensure that young employees are visible to senior management.

■ Recognition and rewards for those senior people who successfully develop leaders.

Evans (1992) argues that the basic tool for developing leaders is cross-functional mobility, ie moving people into jobs where they have to get results through people who have more expertise than themselves. He sounds a note of caution, however, pointing out that in many companies assignments are of too short duration, with the result that managers start things but do not get to see them through. They then fail to develop good implementation skills.

## Other people and relationships

The research evidence here did not point to such clear conclusions. Nevertheless mentoring and coaching are increasingly being used as developmental processes. Obviously the effectiveness of mentoring depends critically on the suitability of the mentor as a role model for a future senior manager and on his or her competence in the mentoring role.

There is evidence that those who get to the top have wider networks of relationships than others. McCauley reports a study in which managers in one corporation were asked to identify those aspects of their relationships with their peers which they had found to be most developmental. The things most often mentioned were:

▌ Sharing information: both technical knowledge and organizational matters.

▌ Comparing career strategies and helping each other learn about career options.

▌ Feedback: helping each other to gain insight into strengths and weaknesses.

## Hardships

The experience of such problems as business failures, expensive mistakes, loss of one's job and other setbacks at work appear in many cases to have had a positive result, ultimately stiffening the individual's resolve and releasing hitherto untapped sources of energy.

McCall, Lombardo and Morrison (1988) point out, however, that the lessons from hardships are mixed and that some people are scarred by them, retreating into denial and cynicism.

## Training programmes

Over the years there has been a rapid growth in executive development programmes: both those offered by external agencies such as business schools and ones offered in-house by large companies. Many of these programmes are specifically designed for 'fast-track' managers or high-flyers. For most, to be sent on one of the longer executive development programmes at one of the major US or European business schools is a clear sign that they are among the chosen élite. Such programmes do offer valuable opportunities for individuals to calibrate themselves against other high-flyers from different cultures as well as from different organizations and there are rich learning opportunities to be garnered by exchanging ideas and experiences with other delegates in addition to any formal learning which takes place in the classroom. The danger, however, is that attendance on such a programme is seen primarily as a rite of passage rather than as a real learning opportunity.

There has been considerable growth in the use of 'expedition' training along the lines pioneered by the Outward Bound Trust. Several UK organizations now offer a similar type of training for junior and middle levels of management, including the Leadership Trust, Endeavour Training and Brathay Hall. The courses offer a variety of physically challenging and adventurous activities such as abseiling, canoeing, rock climbing, orienteering, sailing, etc. The underlying assumption is that the lessons learned in the process of sharing hardships and overcoming stress and fear as a member of a team make participants more effective as leaders. There are several objections to the validity of this approach.

First, the degree of challenge – physical and psychological – naturally varies according to the physique, fitness and other qualities of the participants. For some, the younger and more physically active, who might well spend their weekends and holidays engaged in similar activities, there is virtually no challenge involved. For others, less fit and experienced, the degree of stress experienced may be extreme. Second, the lessons learned during this type of exercise may be more to do with self-knowledge, promotion of self-confidence and ability to work as a member of a team, rather than with leadership as such. Third, there is room to doubt the extent to which the lessons learned transfer easily from the moors and mountains to factories and offices. These courses, although originally aimed at junior and middle-level managers, are increasingly being used in modified form for boards of directors and senior executives.

An alternative approach which has also attracted a large following is the Action Centred Leadership (ACL) course developed by Professor John Adair (1984). Adair was for nine years on the staff of the Royal Military Academy, Sandhurst, where he advised on leadership training. Subsequently he served for a time as Assistant Director of the Industrial Society and, more recently, as Professor of Leadership Studies at the University of Surrey.

Adair describes his approach to leadership as 'functional', distinguishing it from the so-called 'traits' approach and the 'situational' view of leadership. While arguing that there is no one set of qualities or traits which successful leaders share in common, he also holds that certain people seem to possess a general competence to lead effectively in a wide range of different situations, thus dismissing the situational theory. He identifies three basic leadership functions: achievement of task; team maintenance; and meeting individual needs. To achieve these ends the leader must engage in additional functions, such as planning, initiating action, controlling, supporting, informing and evaluating. The ACL programme tends to be used primarily for executives in junior or junior to middle-level appointments.

Templeton College has developed a course for very senior managers, known as the Oxford Strategic Leadership Programme. The programme includes presentations on different aspects, types and theories of leadership; descriptive case studies of the process of bringing about strategic growth and change in organizations; syndicate discussions and team projects; and feedback, both from peers and tutors about individual leadership styles and teamwork. This is a prestigious course, involving top-level practitioners as speakers.

Ashridge Management College has pioneered leadership training in the United Kingdom and between 1982 and 1998 offered a 7-day course known as the Leadership Development Programme, carried out as a franchise operation licensed by the Centre for Creative Leadership, Greensboro, North Carolina. Distinctive features of this programme included:

▌ considerable emphasis on psychometric measurement – participants were required to complete a battery of tests, taking up some 8 hours and covering intelligence, personality, leadership style preferences, vocational interest and aptitude for innovation, before attending the course.

▌ very strong emphasis on personal feedback by highly trained personnel and by peers.

The franchise has now lapsed and in 1999 Ashridge launched its own Leadership Programme, designed in-house.

Ashridge now also offers the Sir Christopher Harding Leadership Programme. Sir Christopher Harding was an outstanding business leader who strongly supported the view that business organizations should face their social and environmental responsibilities. Four companies with which he was closely involved (United Utilities, Consignia, BT, and British Nuclear Fuels) have come together to create the Christopher Harding Legacy Project, the purpose of which is to create a special kind of development opportunity for tomorrow's leaders. The programme is designed to provide participants with:

▌ a tangible vision of values-based leadership;

▌ the skills to make a real difference to their organization and society;

▌ a practical opportunity to bring about a positive dialogue, with organizations seeking to improve the well-being of people in local communities.

The participants are drawn from business, the public sector and the voluntary sector. The programme is in three parts. First, during a residential phase of one week, there is a mix of skills development, inputs on the changing roles of government, business and civil society, and visits to organizations that benefit from outstanding leadership skills. The second phase involves participants working together in small teams to undertake a 100-hour consultancy assignment for a voluntary sector organization. Finally, during a further short residential phase participants will share their learning experiences and establish learning networks to secure their ongoing commitment to the goals of the programme. The programme is carried out by Ashridge Management College's Centre for Business and Society.

The Centre for Leadership Studies at the University of Exeter has offered a Postgraduate Diploma/MA in Leadership since 1993. This is a part-time course that embraces a Diploma, consisting of seven one-week modules spread over two years, followed by an optional one-year MA dissertation. It is designed to help the leadership development of selected individuals, with an age range from late 20s to mid-40s. It includes many of the ingredients of the Templeton College programme, with the focus on the next generation of strategic leaders. Its philosophy is in line with the Inclusive Approach.

In another UK venture, the Leadership Trust Foundation (LTF) and The University of Strathclyde Graduate School of Business (GSB) have together developed a Master of Business Administration degree programme with a specialism in Leadership Studies (MBA/LS). The programme uses a combination of tutor-supported distance (open) learning, formal courses, experiential learning workshops and project work.

The core curriculum of the Strathclyde MBA, which covers the usual business functions, business strategy and strategic thinking, is supplemented by enhancement of participants' self-awareness, self-control and self-confidence through experiential learning in practical leadership and teamwork situations. The development of practical leadership skills takes place at the outdoor leadership development centre of the LTF, at Ross-on-Wye.

A leadership development programme that focuses specifically on sustainable development is Young Canadian Leaders for a Sustainable Future (YCLSF). This programme is sponsored by the International Institute for Sustainable Development (IISD). IISD's goal in regard to leadership development is 'to provide young people with the substantive knowledge, communications skills, resources and practical experience necessary to develop international sustainable development policies and to become effective agents of change. This programme will give young Canadian leaders the skills and opportunities to shape their world'. The programme includes a two-week training session on building sustainable futures in Winnipeg, a six- to eight-month international work placement and a one-week career enhancement session in Winnipeg after completing the placement.

The Foundation for Business and Sustainable Development is a non-profit institution that was set up in 1996 by the World Business Council for Sustainable Development to promote the business understanding of sustainable development and to encourage education and competence building, research and demonstration projects in the field of sustainable development. The Foundation has, with the help of the University of Cambridge, since 1998 worked on a concept called the 'Virtual University' – a structured distance learning framework built primarily for Internet use. The Foundations' objective is to use this concept to introduce an operational understanding of sustainable development. The courses offered include:

█ Corporate Social Responsibility;

█ Sustainable Business Challenge;

█ Global Scenario Challenge.

*Beyond Grey Pinstripes: Preparing MBAs for social and environmental stewardship* (2001) is a joint report of the World Resources Institute (WRI) and the Initiative for Social Responsibility through Business (ISRB), a programme of the Aspen Institute. As a rapidly growing number of businesses discover sources of competitive advantage in social and environmental stewardship, the report identifies the pioneering US Business Schools and faculty 'dedicated to educating future managers to handle complex social issues and provide stewardship of fragile environmental resources'. The Beyond Grey Pinstripes survey was sent to the 313 North American graduate business schools accredited by the International Association for Management Education. Responses were received from 110 schools, with 60 reporting activity on environmental and/or social topics.

One of the top-rated schools was the University of Michigan Business School. All MBA students at Michigan gain basic awareness and knowledge about the importance of healthy social and natural communities for sustainable human development via a compulsory pre-term community citizenship field experience and related seminars, a constant stream of public lectures and panels, assorted modules within required core courses, action-learning projects in the field with non-profit organizations, a required ethics/governance course, and innovative initiatives arising from student organizations. MBAs who wish to acquire deeper/broader insights and skills regarding the management of relations between business, nature and society can pursue a broad array of relevant elective courses with the School, co-listed courses offered in other parts of the university, and various Certificate programmes (eg in Industrial Ecology). Finally, students who wish to orient their career to becoming leader of an organization dedicated to ecological and social sustainability can seek admittance into a highly selective 3-year dual degree programme, such as the Corporate Environment Management Program (CEMP), leading to both an MBA and an MS in Natural Resources/Environment. CEMP develops future private and public leaders possessing the requisite mix of scientific literacy, global vision, entrepreneurial creativity and management skills needed to achieve sustainable commerce and governance. CEMP students are trained to deal with complex social, ecological and economic interdependencies via an emphasis on transdisciplinary approaches, systems thinking, public–private partnerships, and experiential learning in the field.

In the United Kingdom the findings of a research project by the National Council for Education in Management and Leadership were published under the title *Leadership Development: Best practice guide for organizations* (2001). The researchers looked at leadership development 'best practice' in a number of 'blue-chip' companies with a strong UK base. They found that while there was no single strategy that would ensure good practice, there were nine principles that characterized best practice. They grouped these under three headings as follows:

1.  Strategic imperatives:

    ▮ Leadership development, to be effective, must be driven from the top with specialist support.

    ▮ It should be designed to support and drive the business.

    ▮ Consideration should be given to the leadership concept (eg 'hero-type leadership or team leadership), cultural differences and different approaches to development.

2.  Strategic choices:

    ▮ An articulated framework for career development.

    ▮ Variable amounts of formal and informal development.

■ 'Grow your own' senior people or hire them in.

■ The value of competency frameworks and performance management.

■ Retention and reward strategies.

3. Evaluation:

■ An explicit and shared evaluation process.

In-house programmes vary greatly. At one extreme lies the very traditional type of company staff college which is a powerful instrument for perpetuating the existing conventional wisdom and managerial culture. At the other extreme there are in-house programmes which act as major forces for change and organization renewal. One UK financial services company runs an in-house high-flyers programme which involves the participants in developing an alternative strategy for the business. Following the course they are given the opportunity to debate strategic direction with the company's board of directors, the debate being chaired by a neutral management expert from outside the business.

Leadership training programmes have some serious flaws. Many of them are more about management skills than they are about leadership, focusing on things like objective setting or management by objectives. Also, employers make the mistake of believing that training programmes will, by themselves, develop leaders. Leadership development must start at the point of recruitment. Job experiences, rewards and organization cultures must be combined with training to foster leadership potential and encourage the acquisition of the requisite skills.

The whole culture of business needs to change to become more nourishing in respect of creativity and vision. The business schools, too, need to place more emphasis on the social sciences and the humanities.

Nevins and Stumpf (1999) argue that the traditional learning methods most commonly employed in leadership training provide learning experiences that are inadequate in several respects, including:

1. They fail to provide accurate, timely feedback in the areas most critical for success. Feedback enables people to update their expectations regarding the outcomes of their future actions. The timeliness of feedback is important. The value of computer-based learning results in part from the way it can provide immediate feedback. The growing use of 360-degree feedback in work organizations provides vitally important information on how others see one's leadership

style and effectiveness. Simulations, role-playing and other experiential activities provide opportunities for peers, instructors and
observers to provide timely feedback.

2.  They should include lifelike situations, including crises, for learning
    under pressure (similar to state-of-the-art flight simulators for
    pilots). The invention of complex, behaviourally focused leadership
    simulations such as war games has helped to reduce this gap in
    leadership development. Such simulations involve intensive, inter-
    active experiences that recreate organizational life in important
    decision-making groups. They generate leadership behaviours that
    are easily recalled by participants and observed by a trained staff,
    facilitating later review and discussions.

3.  They should permit problem solving and issue diagnosis as a central
    part of the experience. Much of the challenge is in providing a
    partially defined yet still ambiguous situation for learners to tackle.

4.  They should use master–apprentice relationships in the learning
    process so as to guide an effective ongoing development process.
    'Business educators in formal educational programmes are rarely
    masters of business. Their ability to develop students as apprentices
    is minimal, and their interest in doing so is often equally low. In
    contrast with other professions, one might be led to believe that
    management is something that need not be known in order to be
    taught. Medicine, dentistry and the performing arts – among other
    professions – seem to have made a different assumption. A signif-
    icant degree of personal mastery is necessary for the key skills and
    concepts to be passed from one person (the master) to another (the
    apprentice). Formal business education's reliance on books, lectures
    and instructors who do not practice what they teach is a weakness
    of many leadership development courses.

5.  They should challenge a participant on the development programme
    by placing him or her on the firing line to succeed or fail based on
    decisions and actions (consider survival training for the military or
    difficult developmental assignments for multinational executives).

Significant life events, particularly those that are unexpected and personally threatening, have the ability to create years of learning in only a few
moments. Some unexpected events are disasters that start people thinking
again about the safety of others and the environment. Other unexpected
events are less severe – they may be breaks from ways people have done

things in the past, or they may be events that go beyond the responsible parties' ability to forecast. Effective professional development in the future will focus less on rote learning of tools and study of cases, and more on experiences that guide the learners to ask such questions as what can go wrong? And what might the situation be if we projected the current information out 15 years? (Nevins and Stumpf, 1999)

# SELF-DEVELOPMENT

Increasingly high-flyers are taking charge of their own careers and assuming responsibility for their own development. This can involve, at the extreme, taking a career break to study an MBA degree. For many it now means part-time study for a degree or diploma. Now that few organizations can offer a 'cradle to the grave' career, high-flyers expect their journey to the top to involve working for several organizations rather than one. Given this prospect they can clearly not just sit around waiting to be developed. Access to open learning systems has greatly increased the opportunities for self-development.

Another factor encouraging young managers to concern themselves with their own development is the increasing tendency for organizations to become flatter and reduce the number of levels in the hierarchy, thus reducing the number of career steps and giving rise to the paradox of 'high-flyers and low ceilings'.

# DERAILMENT

The research team at the Center for Creative Leadership (Lombardo, 1988) have also made a particular study of the process of *executive derailment* which happens when someone who was assessed as having the potential to go right to the top fails to do so. In one early study 19 top executives who had taken action to derail a high-flyer gave their reasons. These included issues to do with personal qualities such as insensitivity to others, arrogance or betrayal of trust as well as managerial incompetence or inability to think strategically. Later studies identified six specific clusters of flaws associated with derailment:

▌ Problems with personal relationships.

▌ Difficulty in moulding staff.

▌ Difficulty in making the transition to a strategic level.

▌ Lack of follow through.

▌ Over-dependence on a particular boss.

▌ Inability to handle differences with higher management.

The researchers suggest the following as ways and means of reducing the incidence of derailment:

▌ Improve the level of understanding of the requirements for real success in high-level jobs.

▌ Improve the ability of the organization to assess and develop the competencies, skills or other attributes that match these requirements.

▌ Create an environment in which learning is taken seriously.

▌ Provide more support and counselling when managers reach critical points in their careers.

▌ Plan career development so as to avoid late surprises.

## ISSUES AND PROBLEMS IN THE MANAGEMENT OF HIGH-FLYERS

In addition to such problems as the self-fulfilling prophecy referred to previously the research in this field has identified a number of other commonly encountered problems or issues as follows:

▌ Those who are missed by the system of assessment and not included in the high-flyers group – particularly those who fail only marginally to win inclusion – may become resentful and lose motivation or leave the organization altogether.

▌ If the high-flyers are promoted too rapidly they may not stay in any one job long enough for any real learning to take place or for valid feedback to become available. It will also be difficult to make a valid assessment of their performance.

■ There is a very real danger that although high-flyers are deemed to be a corporate resource, local, national or divisional managers may try to hold on to their best young managers rather than offer them up to the overall company pool of talent.

■ The increasing need for future top managers in international businesses to have had international experience is sometimes difficult to meet in this day and age when managers, whether male or female, have spouses or partners with their own careers with different locational requirements.

■ Expectations are created which become impossible to fulfil. This tendency was marked in the UK in the early 1990s when, in conditions of severe recession and consequent cutbacks in industry and commerce, it was often impossible for companies to honour promises of exceptional career progress given in the buoyant years of the 1980s.

■ Companies often fail to provide adequate routes for young professional, scientific or technical specialists to join high-flyers programmes alongside those who have been recruited specifically as management trainees. Sir Richard Sykes, former Chief Executive, Glaxo Smith Kline, began his working career as a laboratory assistant in Halifax Royal Infirmary. A young laboratory worker today would not easily gain access to a high flyers programme in any major chemical or pharmaceutical company irrespective of his or her potential.

## COPING WITH STRESS

Young people on the high-flyers programme are often under considerable pressure. This can lead to 'burn-out' or some other reaction to stress. As the level of the leader's responsibility rises, so the degree of stress experienced may rise accordingly. Kets de Vries (1994) has listed some of the pressures which create stress for those who lead, including loneliness and the loss of a network of supportive peer relationships, coping with the possible envy or rivalry of others and the pressure to keep on delivering success can bring its own pressures.

Other sources of pressure identified by Sadler (1988) include status anxiety (wanting simultaneously to be respected and popular); the difficulty in maintaining a strong sense of personal identity in face of strong expectations from followers; and the problem of learning when to say 'No' and achieve a balance between work and home. The symptoms of stress are often visible to those close to the leader; they include drinking to excess, paranoid symptoms, sudden violent rages, sweating and stomach disorders.

Heifetz (1994) suggests seven ways in which leaders, as part of their self-development, can deal with stress:

▌ Take time out to reflect, look at the wider picture, try to see events as a spectator, not a participant.

▌ Distinguish self from role. Do not take the inevitable criticism as a personal affront.

▌ Externalize conflict, concentrate on the issues, not the personalities.

▌ Use allies. Do not try to exercise leadership alone. Gain support from mentors and confidants.

▌ Listen to yourself and become fully self-aware. Watch out for yourself engaging in special pleading or distorting information.

▌ Find a sanctuary – a place and a time where you can get away from it all and recharge your batteries.

▌ Keep your sense of purpose. Hold on to the vision despite setbacks and opposition.

## SUMMARY

The most effective processes for developing leaders appear to be a mix of the following:

▌ Challenging job assignments early on in the individual's career which call on the use of influence rather than position power in order to get results.

▌ Feedback mechanisms such as 360° appraisals which enable the individual to take an objective view about his or her effectiveness in a leadership role and to take action accordingly. When this feedback is given in the context of a leadership training programme it can be particularly open and objective without damaging the individual's relationships with co-workers.

▌ Self-awareness which comes partly from receptiveness to feedback but which, in addition calls for a genuine concern for self-development and a desire to improve.

▌ Supportive relationships with mentors who can act as role models, 'confessors' and critics.

# 8

# Cultural differences and diversity

In every aspect of leadership studies there are contradictory or ambiguous findings. This is particularly the case in respect of cross-cultural studies.

## THE AMERICAN BIAS

Smith (1992) points out that the best-known models of leadership have been developed in the US where the notion that there is one best way of leading has received little support. In consequence, US academics have developed complex contingency theories such as Fiedler's to account for how different styles are suited to different situations. In other cultural settings, however, where there is much less emphasis on individualism, such as Japan, Taiwan, India, Iran and Brazil, the notion of a single, effective leadership style has received more support. In all these countries, studies have shown that effective leaders are those who give equal emphasis to the task and to the needs of employees. Results from Western European countries and from Russia, where individualism is stronger, are in line with those from the US, indicating that an effective leadership style is a function of the situation. Smith wisely stresses that the interpretation of cross-cultural studies is plagued with difficulties. In collectivist countries like Japan the conventional dichotomy of autocratic and participative management does not fit well with a culture in which leadership is frequently both autocratic and participative at the same time.

# DIMENSIONS OF CULTURAL DIFFERENCE

A pioneer in the field of cultural differences and their implications for styles of leadership is Hofstede (1991). He compares national cultures in terms of their differences on four dimensions:

▌ Power distance:

– the extent to which a society accepts the fact that power in organizations is distributed unequally.

▌ Uncertainty avoidance:

– the extent to which a society feels threatened by uncertain and ambiguous situations and tries to avoid these by establishing rules and believing in absolute truth.

▌ Individualism versus collectivism:

– individualism implies a loosely knit social framework in which people are supposed to take care of themselves and of their immediate families only, while collectivism is characterized by a tight social framework in which people can expect to be looked after by the community and in return give it their loyalty and commitment.

▌ Masculinity versus femininity:

– the extent to which the dominant values in society are masculine (eg assertiveness, acquisitiveness, disregard for quality of life issues, etc).

To give some examples, countries scoring high on power distance include the Philippines, Venezuela, Mexico, Yugoslavia, Singapore and India, while low scoring countries are Denmark, Austria, Israel, New Zealand and Ireland.

Countries scoring highly on uncertainty avoidance are Greece, Portugal, Belgium, Japan, Peru, France and Yugoslavia, while countries with low scores on this dimension include Singapore, Denmark, Sweden, Hong Kong, Ireland and the UK.

Highly individualistic cultures exist in Australia, the US, the UK, The Netherlands, Canada and New Zealand, while Pakistan, Columbia, Venezuela, Thailand, Peru, Taiwan and Singapore are strongly collectivist.

The most strongly masculine cultures are to be found in Japan, Austria, Venezuela, Mexico, Italy, Ireland, Columbia and South Africa, while the least masculine occur in Sweden, Norway, Denmark, The Netherlands and Yugoslavia.

Hofstede, like Smith, points out that leadership theories current in the management literature have largely originated in the US. This country is characterised by an average level of power distance, extremely strong individualism, slightly below average uncertainty avoidance and slightly above average masculinity. He argues that many US-based theories of leadership advocate that leaders should encourage participation in decision making on the part of their subordinates but on the basis that the initiative towards participation is taken by the leader. This makes sense from the middle position of the US on the power distance scale. A stronger power distance culture would have resulted in theories emphasizing the use of power and manipulation. Hofstede exemplifies this point by citing French management writing which pays little attention to participation but focuses strongly on the exercise of power. On the other hand, in countries like Sweden, Norway and Israel, with low power distance scores, there is greater acceptance of models of leadership behaviour in which the initiatives are taken by subordinates.

Different approaches to participation involve differences in uncertainty avoidance. In Sweden, steps towards industrial democracy began with local experiments, reflecting low uncertainty avoidance, whereas in Germany, where uncertainty avoidance is strong, industrial democracy was established by legislation.

Hofstede emphasises that leaders cannot choose their styles at will. What is feasible depends to a large extent on the cultural conditioning of their subordinates. US writers such as McGregor, Likert and Blake have tended, nevertheless, to be prescriptive, favouring a leadership style that fits the culture of the US and centres such as Canada and Australia but not countries with larger power distance cultures. One leadership theorist singled out by Hofstede as allowing for a certain amount of cultural relativity is Fiedler (see Chapter 5) who argues that different leadership styles are needed for 'difficult' and 'easy' situations and that a cultural gap between superior and subordinates is one of the factors that make for difficulty. Hofstede suggests that managers moving from low power distance societies to ones characterized by high power distance soon learn that they have to behave more autocratically if they are to be effective. He goes on to assert that the Western colonial power with the highest power distance – France – has enjoyed and still enjoys the best relationship with its ex-colonies and that a possible reason is that real autocrats are more acceptable in the Third World than leaders who adopt an autocratic stance which is at variance with their national character.

## Seven dimensions of cultural difference

Trompenaars and Hampden-Turner (2001) distinguish seven dimensions of cultural difference, which, they claim, account for the major differences between national cultures. The dimensions are:

▌ rule-making or universalism versus exception finding or particularism;

▌ self-interest or individualism versus group interest or communitarianism;

▌ preference for precise processes or specificity versus preference for patterned processes or diffusion;

▌ inhibiting the emotions versus giving expression to them;

▌ earning status through achievements versus earning status derived from family or education (ascriptive);

▌ inner directed versus outer directed;

▌ time seen as a sequential process versus time seen in terms of synchronicity.

Hampden-Turner and Trompenaars (1993) reached the conclusion that Swedish companies, particularly the large ones, were able to draw on extraordinary qualities of leadership. They cite Gyllenhammar of Volvo, Barnevik of ABB, Svedberg of Ericsson and Carlzon of SAS, among others, as examples. They present three league tables, one on managerial initiative, one on the extent to which leaders delegate and one on the capacity of leaders to take a long-term view. Sweden is given the highest score on the first two of these and is in third place, behind Japan and Germany on the third. The United Kingdom is ranked 20th out of 22 countries on managerial initiative, 15th on delegation and 17th on the capacity to take a long-term view.

# A COMPARATIVE STUDY OF ATTITUDES TO LEADERSHIP IN DIFFERENT COUNTRIES

Sadler and Hofstede (1976) carried out a cross-cultural research study using the classification of leadership styles developed by Tannenbaum and Schmidt as described in Chapter 5. They examined the *preferences* and *perceptions* of leadership style in different countries. All the respondents in the study were employed by IBM, thus holding the influence of corporate culture constant.

Studies were carried out in 55 countries in all. In some cases all the employees of this company were surveyed, in others the survey was confined to people in particular jobs. In order to carry out the survey, 14 language versions of the original English language questionnaire were prepared.

The *preferences* expressed by personnel working in marketing and service organizations of the company (*n* = 19,383) were as follows:

| | |
|---|---|
| 'Tells' (autocratic) | 3% |
| 'Sells' (persuasive) | 25% |
| 'Consults' (consultative) | 56% |
| 'Joins' (democratic) | 16% |
| No reply or invalid | 5% |

The *perceptions* of the same population were as follows:

| | |
|---|---|
| 'Tells' | 17% |
| 'Sells' | 31% |
| 'Consults' | 30% |
| 'Joins' | 7% |
| 'None of these' | 14% |
| No reply or invalid | 6% |

As in the UK study the leadership style perceived by the employees was related to their expressed level of job satisfaction and satisfaction with the company as an employer. In Britain it had been shown that it was the group of employees who answered, 'My manager does not correspond at all closely to any of these four styles' who were the least satisfied with their jobs and the company. This result was replicated with great regularity in the other countries surveyed.

In the UK study, among those who did perceive a clear-cut leadership style, the highest levels of satisfaction were found in those who perceived their manager as consultative and the lowest among those perceiving the 'tells' or autocratic style. In the international survey, however, there were considerable differences both between countries and between job categories in which perceived leadership style was associated with the highest levels of satisfaction.

In the international survey three questions were used to evaluate the relationship between employees and their managers:

1.   How satisfied are you with your working relationship with your manager?

2.   How much confidence do you have in your immediate manager?

3.   All in all, how good a job is being done by your immediate manager?

Taking the sample as a whole, the most favourable responses on all three questions were given by those who perceived the 'consults' style, followed by those perceiving 'sells'. Those perceiving 'joins' scored favourably on working relationship and level of confidence but unfavourably on, 'How good a job. . .?' Those perceiving 'none of these styles' score the lowest of all.

## Comparing country and job differences

In order to measure differences between countries, comparisons were made only between groups of people in the same jobs. Conversely, in order to measure differences between jobs, comparisons were made only between people in the same country.

One analysis compared each of five job categories – data processing salespersons, systems analysts, maintenance engineers, data centre employees and administrative staff – for each of four countries: the UK, Japan, Brazil and Australia. This sub-sample totalled 6029 employees. In order to measure the country effect, weighted averages over jobs were taken, giving each job equal weight.

A second study of country differences compared the UK, Germany and France. In this case the job groups were engineers, technicians and administrative staff in product development laboratories. Here the sample totalled 1256.

The results of both inter-country comparisons showed that the differences between countries were more pronounced in respect of preferences than perceptions. As might be expected, the greatest differences in perceptions were between those countries with the most marked differences in culture, such as the UK, Japan and Brazil. There emerged three main groupings of preferences:

1. An above average preference for the relatively authoritarian 'sells' style and a below average preference for the consultative style: Japan.

2. A group with a high peak of preferences for the consultative style: Australia, the UK and Germany.

3. An above average preference for the 'joins' style and a below average preference for the consultative style: Brazil and France.

Actual leadership behaviour as perceived by the respondents was found to be much more similar from country to country.

# A EUROPEAN STYLE OF LEADERSHIP – MYTH OR REALITY?

Wills (1996) set out to explore the question of whether or not the concept of a distinctively European style of leadership is myth or reality. Starting from the position that the vast majority of studies of leadership have originated within the American culture – and American academic culture at that – he set out to ascertain the ideas and attitudes of European managers. He used a structured interview format to obtain the views of 25 European managers in 14 countries.

The first finding to emerge from analysis of the interviews was the extent of the differences between these managers, in terms of their values, assumptions and opinions. These differences reflected the varying cultural backgrounds of the respondents. At one extreme – for example, in the replies of a French and a Belgian manager – was the view that management and leadership were much the same. 'Managers and leaders for me are the same thing.' At the other extreme were views typified by the remark, 'A leader is someone who is a cut above management'. Although the respondents' ideas about the nature of leadership varied considerably, there was more agreement on the notion that leadership is a reciprocal process that occurs between the leader and followers and that the ways in which followers treat their leaders affects the way that their leaders behave towards them.

When invited to talk about the major issues currently facing European business leaders, the interviewees displayed a great deal of commonality in their replies. There were three broad areas of concern:

■ Issues at the level of the individual.

■ Bridging issues.

■ Issues at the social level.

At the level of the individual, the issues raised were to do with the personal characteristics of successful leaders. One was the issue of morality and ethical behaviour, the importance of being able to trust the leader, believe in him or her. Related ideas were the need for consistency and reliability on the part of the leader and the quality of empathy, defined as the ability to express what people themselves feel instinctively to be the right thing.

A second issue to emerge at the individual level was the nature of empowerment – a much used and abused term – but taken here to mean 'the act of strengthening an individual's beliefs in his or her sense of effectiveness'. The views of a number of respondents are summed up as follows: 'The true nature of leadership moves from managing things to generating insight into the art of the possible.'

The third individual leadership issue to come up in discussion was the role of emotion in leadership, the ability to interact with others at an emotional, as distinct from purely intellectual, level. In the words of a Swiss manager, 'It's up to the leader of a company to show that he allows and respects emotion'. The traditional stereotype of the male-dominated 'macho' culture in which the expression of emotion and feelings is taboo was not apparent in the views expressed by this sample.

'Bridging' issues link the individual aspects of leadership with the social. One such is communication. Leaders were seen as people capable of making things clear by using simple words, anecdotes and brevity of expression. At the same time they were able to encourage open, unconstrained debate.

The second 'bridging' issue is visioning. Here visioning is defined as 'creating a new reality'. Leaders need to have a long-term future orientation and to be able to generate a high level of commitment to the achievement of longer term goals. They need to be capable of getting their visions shared at all levels of the organizations.

The third 'bridging' issue is charisma – the ability of a leader to exercise influence by virtue of his or her own beliefs, behaviour and example. Respondents were pessimistic about the possibility of learning to behave in a charismatic way. Nevertheless, there was considerable support for the notion that charisma is not so much an attribute of the personality of the leader as a function of the relationship between leader and followers. In other words, charisma only exists if followers perceive it and behave accordingly. Wills quotes the perceptive comment of Wilson: 'If a man runs down the street proclaiming that he alone can save others from impending doom and if he immediately wins a following, then he is a charismatic leader: a social relationship has come into being. If he does not win a following, he is simply a lunatic.'

Under the heading of social issues, the first is the influence of competitive pressures. The pressure to produce more and more with fewer and fewer people was seen as the greatest challenge to contemporary leaders. Another factor was the globalization of business and the consequent requirement to deal with people of different nationalities and build effective multinational teams, together with the challenge of exercising leadership over great distances.

The final issue was that of change: increasingly seen as the primary function of the leader. Wills concluded from his study that although the analysis of the issues perceived by European leaders would probably not differ greatly from the issues perceived by a sample of American leaders, it would be wrong to assume that they could be resolved by the application of tried and tested American models. The cultural diversity of Europe is much greater than that of North America. Leadership as a concept is not as salient in Europe as it is across the Atlantic nor is it as 'romanticized'.

# THREE EUROPEAN CULTURES

'Leadership in the UK is not the same as leadership in Sweden, France or Spain. To engage in the same behaviours regardless of context is to risk failure and humiliation. To use the same leadership processes without regard to national context is to risk at least mild misunderstanding and private amusement. At worst, it risks a fundamental but unrecognised clash of values which can only rebound to the disadvantage of all parties.' This is the conclusion reached by Durcan (1994), as a result of conducting research in different European countries. He points out that growing up in a particular culture results in the assimilation of a particular set of values and behavioural norms. Moving outside the culture with which one is familiar, the expectations created by this process frequently are not met. Differences of language and concept make it difficult, even in Western Europe, to develop a common understanding of the meaning of leadership. For example, in the UK and the US, it is generally accepted that leadership and management are different, albeit related, processes. Thus it makes sense to offer leadership development programmes as distinct from management development programmes. In Durcan's view, however, in many Western European countries this distinction is not accepted. In the business context, leadership is seen as inseparable from management. Leadership as a separate concept is something one finds in the world of politics, not business.

Durcan gives an account of research carried out by Ashridge Management College into leadership patterns in different European cultures. The results indicated that some countries fell into clusters characterized by similar values and patterns of behaviour. Other countries, such as Germany, were sufficiently distinctive as to defy such attempts at classification.

One cluster – the UK and Ireland – called the Anglo culture was characterized by values and expectations also observable in the US, Canada, Australia and New Zealand. Anglo cultures focus on results. Leadership is seen as a means of achieving desired outcomes such as quality improvements and as the way the leader behaves towards the followers in order to produce these results. It is less likely that leadership will be seen as a process of mutual influence. In Anglo cultures, the prevailing belief is that if the wholehearted commitment of followers is to be secured, the leader must do more than exercise the managerial authority vested in his position. The use of authority may ensure compliance but the achievements of a compliant workforce will fall short of those of one which is committed. Traditionally it was believed that commitment could be achieved through such processes as good communications, by providing opportunities for personal growth and development and by the practices lumped together under the heading of good human relations. More recently it has been accepted that more is needed; in particular the process which has become known as empowerment and the process of creating and articulating an inspiring vision of future possibilities. Followers are motivated through challenges and opportunities which appeal primarily to competitive, aggressive and materialistic values. Another aspect of the Anglo culture is a low regard for structure in the sense of firm schedules and clear rules, preferring a more pragmatic approach, treating each issue on its own merits.

Another cluster links together the Scandinavian countries. These share some values with the Anglo cluster but in one important respect there is a difference which affects their whole approach to leadership. They share a view about the purpose of life which is strikingly different. Instead of the competitive, aggressive materialism of the Anglos, there is a concern for the quality of life generally. For them, leadership is more about relationships than results. 'Leadership is not so much about providing direction or achieving results as about building the kinds of mutual relationships which make achievement possible.'

A third cluster, labelled Mediterranean, comprised Greece, Italy, Spain, Portugal, Turkey and France. In these countries leaders are seen as and expected to be more powerful. The exercise of power carries responsibilities and obligations and involves what is termed 'paternal leadership'. Followership is a response to the power of the leader, that is to say, people follow a leader primarily because of his or her status or position. In this culture there is also a stronger preference for structure than in the Anglo or Scandinavian cultures.

In conclusion, Durcan argues, there is growing evidence to support the view that simply exporting Anglo models of leadership – in person or as concepts – is far from satisfactory. Leadership models need to fit the cultures in which they are to operate.

# LEADING INTERNATIONAL TEAMS

Davison and Ward (1999) have carried out research into the leadership issues involved in working with international teams. They begin by looking at why international teams are now increasingly common in international organizations. Three trends in particular are driving this development. These are: globalization; 'teaming' – the need, in the light of the increased complexities of scientific, medical, environmental and commercial issues, for individuals from different backgrounds and countries to collaborate to resolve problems; and the revolution in information technology, which allows the creation of dispersed international teams.

International teams differ from single-nationality teams because of the additional complexities that stem from such factors as different languages and communication styles, different ways of looking at the world and processing information, different behavioural expectations, and different stereotypes held by team members of each other. These additional complexities demand much greater attention to the team process.

International team leaders need to 'know' their teams and understand the many ways in which cultural differences can affect the interaction in their teams. Davison and Ward suggest that there are five cultural and three organizational factors that can have a significant impact. The cultural factors are: the degree of difference or similarity between the cultural norms of the individuals in the team; the degree to which individuals might manifest their cultural norms; differences in language fluency, communication patterns, non-verbals and who says what, when; culturally different leadership styles; and different expectations about key team processes. The authors rightly warn that nationality is only a rough guide to someone's culture and that national stereotypes tend to be unhelpful, especially when attributed to individuals. The organizational factors are the status of different cultures within the organization; the geographic spread of the team members; and the similarity or difference between the functional and professional 'cultures' represented in the team.

The team leader has to imagine all the possible scenarios of what could actually adversely affect the team's effectiveness and ensure that, right from the start, he or she establishes key patterns of interaction and ground rules that will prevent unhelpful behaviour.

The creation of 'them' and 'us' groups is a potential danger for any team. But three types of inequality can make this problem more pronounced in international teams. Structural inequality occurs when one nationality outnumbers the others. Linguistic inequality occurs when team members have different levels of fluency in the working language and communication norms of that language. The third, and most difficult, type of inequality is when some nationalities see themselves, and are seen, as having more status, power, resources and influence regardless of the truth. These inequalities need to be actively managed. For example, the speed and pattern of speech in the team should give second-language speakers and others who prefer not to start talking when someone else is already talking, time to think and speak. Brainstorming needs to be done in a systematic way that asks for everybody's ideas, rather than just letting people 'shout out' which means that some people may not participate. Everyone must be comfortable with the decision-making process or alternatives must be found.

In the light of all these challenges, the international team leader's role is complex and demanding. He or she must decide how to balance the need for both technical and leadership skills and then match the style of leadership to the strategic and operational needs of each stage of the team's development. The leader must also balance his or her three key roles: managing the team's boundaries with the rest of the organization, managing the team's task, and managing interaction within the team. At the same time, he or she must be particularly careful to keep the overall leadership style in tune with the cultural mix and context of the team.

## COMPETENCIES OF GLOBAL LEADERS

A survey carried out by Andersen Consulting (now Accenture) (1999) identified three competencies of effective global leaders:

▌ Personal mastery – a high degree of self-awareness to monitor their own behaviour, build on their strengths and fill gaps in their competencies. 'The global leader must be trustworthy and be driven by core personal and often spiritual values, possessing in high degree a good balance of emotional, intellectual and business intelligence. . . Superficial development of leadership skills will not suffice.'

▌ Providing organizational leadership by creating internal and external networks of influence, including alliances and partnerships as well as formal acquisitions and mergers. 'Since no one individual will be able to manage single-handedly the high degree of complexity created by multiple networks, the leadership must be shared.'

▌ Building organizational and individual competence by seeking and using differences of thought, style and culture around the globe.

   Interviewees were asked to score the importance of 14 competencies under the headings of 'the past', 'the present' and 'the future'. The greatest differences in scores between the past and the future were for:

- thinks globally;

- appreciates cultural diversity;

- lives the values;

- builds teamwork and partnerships.

## DEVELOPING GLOBAL LEADERS

McCall and Hollenbeck (2002) assert that, while approaches to global strategy and structure have become increasingly sophisticated, our understanding of the kinds of leaders required in such a complex setting has remained simple and simplistic. We intuitively know that leading in an international context is more difficult than doing it on home ground and that it requires more sophisticated skills, but we are less sure about what that means for how we develop effective international leaders.

They set out the following principles for developing global leaders:

1.  Business strategy drives development. Quite simply, business strategy and the structure of a global corporation directly affect how many and what kinds of international jobs exist, how many global executives with what kinds of skills are needed, and what experiences are available to teach them what they need to know.

2.  What global leaders need to know can be learned, but it's not all business. Business is business wherever you are. Once beyond that core, however, the cultural context in which the business takes place has a profound effect on the content of the lessons learned. Many business lessons can be learned without expatriation, but most cultural adaptability lessons cannot.

3.  Global executives learn their trade the same way that other executives do. The basic process of learning is the same regardless of the executive's country of origin or whether the development is for global, expatriate or local executive work. If you give talented people challenging and relevant experiences, if they are open to learning from their experience, and if they get the necessary support, then they can learn many of the lessons needed. Trying to run a business in a country significantly different from one's own is an experience for which there is no substitute. Doing it a second time, in a quite different culture, can be transformational.

4.  There is no magic bullet for developing global executives. When working internationally there are many more variables impacting success or failure. An organization cannot 'make' people develop, even when it 'knows' what they need. Most of the forces that influence the development of global executives are not under an organization's direct control. It is therefore all the more important to do well at whatever is realistically within the organization's sphere.

5.  A global executive is not a single thing. Firms operating internationally need leaders who have one thing in common: they must all be capable of working outside of their home countries. But, not all global jobs are alike. There are many different types of global corporations, many different strategies for doing global business, and many different structures.

6.   Global careers are hazardous. Going global adds significantly to the possibility of career derailment. Although global executives are in general more talented than their domestic counterparts, they are also more susceptible to things going wrong because of numerous contextual and organizational factors. International work has many more critical danger points – going out, coming back, working for a boss from a different culture, etc. These changes offer greater possibilities for learning but also greater opportunities to fail.

7.   Developing global executives is more complicated and uncertain than its domestic counterpart, but it is not impossible. The problem is that with the complexity and risk, few organizations have adopted a model robust enough for the challenge and then committed the time and resources necessary to implement it.

8.   Global executives must take much more responsibility for their own development. Individuals with global aspirations must seek out international exposure, not wait for it to find them, and the earlier the better.

In answer to the question what skills, abilities and values do global managers need, McCall and Hollenbeck give the following suggestions:

▌   how to work with cultures different from one's own;

▌   how to run a business that is international in scope;

▌   how to lead and manage people unlike oneself;

▌   how to handle a complex array of often difficult relationships;

▌   how to develop the skills and attitudes necessary for effective personal behaviour;

▌   how to know oneself to preserve and enhance one's family relationships and to manage one's own career.

# GENDER DIFFERENCES

The literature on leadership has a strongly masculine ring to it. Most lists of outstanding business leaders are exclusively male and many writers exclusively use masculine pronouns. In today's world, however, as equal opportunity continues its slow advance, more and more women are assuming leadership roles and a select few are actually making it to the top. In Britain, the best-known female role models, such as Anita Roddick of Body Shop or Dame Steve Shirley of Xansa are entrepreneurs who have built up their own business. Women chief executives, such as Marjorie Sciardino of the Pearson Group, who have made it to the top of a public company are still relatively rare – at this level the glass ceiling is still difficult to break through.

Women who wish to develop their ability to lead as well as manage may find it useful to study the careers of these and other successful women who have got to the top, but they are more likely to learn about such things as balancing working life with domestic responsibilities and relationships than they are to gain insight into leadership issues.

It is, of course, important that companies should do their best to remove the invisible barriers that prevent many women from advancing to top-level leadership roles. Arrangements in respect of maternity leave may be satisfactory, but there are so many other factors that act as negative influences, such as calling breakfast meetings or expecting managers to put in long hours, thus making difficulties for working parents.

## Male and female leadership styles

Hooijberg and DiTomaso (1996) have summarized the main research findings on differences in leadership style between men and women. A number of studies found little difference. They quote findings by Bass (1992), for example, who found that once women have attained leadership positions they behave in very similar ways to men in such positions. Another study, which analysed 17 pieces of research on the subject, also found no differences. One reason suggested for this finding is that women who pursue managerial careers differ from women who do not. Some other studies did, however, find differences. In these, women were seen to use a more democratic, participative approach, compared to a more autocratic, directive style used by men.

There is also some evidence that sex stereotypes influence the way in which male and female leaders are evaluated as to their effectiveness. In one case an experiment showed that female leaders received more negative responses than males, even though they put forward the same suggestions and arguments. The assumption that the leader is in control and knows the answers is frequently construed as a particularly masculine notion.

Morrison, White and Van Velsor (1987) studied the careers of 78 of the most senior women in corporate America. The popular literature and some earlier social science research had prepared them to expect to find a distinctive feminine style of leadership, characterized by greater willingness to listen, and being more empathetic and people oriented and less aggressive in the pursuit of goals compared with males. However, they did not find any significant differences between men's and women's styles.

Some other studies did, however, find differences. In these, women were seen to use a more democratic, participative approach, compared with a more autocratic, directive style used by men. Rosener (1990), for example, found women not only encouraged participation and shared power and information to a greater extent than men, they went further still, practising what she calls *interactive leadership,* which involves enhancing the feelings of self-worth of others, believing that high levels of performance result from people feeling excited about their work and good about themselves.

Jan Grant (1992) suggests there are six qualities which woman can bring to the leadership role:

■ Communication and cooperation – finding ways of bringing about conciliation and resolving conflict.

■ Affiliation and attachment. Valuing relationships with others over self advancement.

■ Power. Seeing power not as a means of dominating others but as something to be used on behalf of the community.

■ Physicality. Women's physical makeup, with its emphasis on pregnancy and giving birth 'grounds women on the day to day realities of growth and development'.

■ Emotionality, vulnerability and lack of self-confidence, Women can more easily express their emotions, their vulnerability and self-doubts, and can more accurately assess their own strengths and weaknesses.

■ Intimacy and nursing. Having greater capacity for empathy with others and able to get closer.

# SUMMARY

The greater part of the research and writing on leadership in modern times has originated in the United States and carries with it an inevitable cultural bias.

Hofstede and Trompenaars with Hampden-Turner have studied the differences between national cultures and their implications for leader behaviour and the factors making for effective leadership. Hofstede emphasizes that leaders cannot choose their leadership styles at will. What is feasible depends on the cultural conditioning of their subordinates.

Other writers have studied similarities and differences between leadership styles in the different European countries. Wills concluded that the cultural diversity of Europe is much greater than that of North America and that generalizations about a European style of management are groundless. Durcan, too, found that 'Leadership in the UK is not the same as leadership in Sweden, France or Spain'.

Increasingly, leaders find themselves in the position of leading international teams. Such teams differ from single-nationality teams because of the additional complexities that stem from such factors as different languages and communication styles, different ways of looking at the world and processing information, different behavioural expectations, and different stereotypes held by team members of each other. These additional complexities demand much greater attention to the team process.

While approaches to global strategy and structure have become increasingly sophisticated, our understanding of the kinds of leaders required in such a complex setting has remained simple and simplistic. We intuitively know that leading in an international context is more difficult than doing it on home ground and that it requires more sophisticated skills, but we are less sure about what that means for how we develop effective international leaders.

Among the key skills needed by international leaders are the following:

■ how to work with cultures different from one's own;

■ how to run a business that is international in scope;

■ how to lead and manage people unlike oneself;

▪ how to handle a complex array of often difficult relationships;

▪ how to develop the skills and attitudes necessary for effective personal behaviour;

▪ how to know oneself to preserve and enhance one's family relationships and to manage one's own career.

## Gender issues

The literature on leadership has a strongly masculine ring to it. Most lists of outstanding business leaders are exclusively male and many writers exclusively use masculine pronouns. In today's world, however, as equal opportunity continues its slow advance, more and more women are assuming leadership roles.

A review of the main research findings on differences in leadership style between men and women reveals that a number of studies found little difference. They quote Bass, for example, who found that once women have attained leadership positions they behave in very similar ways to men in such positions. Another study, which analysed 17 pieces of research on the subject, also found no differences. One reason suggested for this finding is that women who pursue managerial careers differ from women who do not.

Some other studies did, however, find differences. In these, women were seen to use a more democratic, participative approach, compared with a more autocratic, directive style used by men. One such study found women not only encouraged participation and shared power and information to a greater extent than men, they went further still, practising *interactive leadership*, which involves enhancing the feelings of self-worth of others, believing that high levels of performance result from people feeling excited about their work and good about themselves.

# 9

# Role models

What follows is my own personal selection of leadership role models, chosen to reflect a wide range of styles, values and approaches. Two are drawn from industry, one from politics and one from the military. The latter, William Slim, has served for me personally as a role model ever since, as a young man, I read his account of the war in Burma.

## WILLIAM SLIM – A ROLE MODEL FOR WAR AND PEACE

According to Dixon (1976), Field Marshal Lord Slim was loved by his army perhaps more than any other commander has been loved by his men since Nelson. In his account of the victorious Burma campaign (Slim, 1956), he set out his philosophy and approach to leadership.

The 14th Army, when he assumed command, was defeated and demoralised, lacking even the most basic amenities, and feeling isolated from home, not just in distance but in terms of feeling ignored and insignificant. The troops called themselves 'the Forgotten Army'. On taking up his new duties, Slim sat down quietly to think through ways and means of raising their morale. He defined it as 'that intangible force which will move a whole group of men to give their last ounce to achieve something without counting the cost to themselves; that makes them feel they are part of something greater than themselves'. He reached the conclusion that morale, if it was to endure, needed three foundations: *spiritual*, *intellectual* and *material*.

His spiritual foundation is very close to what today, in business circles, is referred to as a sense of mission. It involves having a worthwhile objective and feeling that what one does contributes directly to its achievement. The intellectual factor is to do with credibility of the objective – it is something that can be reached – and confidence in the organization and in its leaders. The material element involves such matters as believing that one is being fairly treated, that as far as possible one is well equipped for the task in hand and that living and working conditions are as good as circumstances permit.

Slim saw that the only way to instil a sense of mission into half a million men was by a direct approach to the men themselves. 'Not by written exhortations, not by wireless talks, but by informal talks and contacts between troops and commanders.' Slim and his senior officers talked to whole units, to collections of officers, to headquarters staff, to little groups of men and to individual soldiers casually encountered. Slim personally addressed every combatant unit, usually standing on the bonnet of his jeep, often doing as many as three or four such speeches in a day. Also, to convince those in the less spectacular or less evidently vital supporting roles of their importance, Slim and his commanders made visits to these units both to show interest in their activities and to tell them how the fighting units depended on them. He also tried to keep everyone, regardless of rank, informed about the general situation.

In order to build credibility and to convince the troops that victory over the Japanese was possible, he adopted two approaches. First, he placed considerable emphasis on patrolling, a process through which the men learned the ways of the jungle and developed the ability to move through it with confidence and to secure a large number of small victories against the enemy. Stories of these successes spread rapidly and lost nothing in the telling. The second technique involved a number of minor offensives in which the 14th Army was always in greatly preponderating strength, thus minimising the risk of failure. Gradually, the belief grew stronger – the Japanese *could* be defeated.

On the material front, Slim's leadership style was well illustrated by the fact that when any of the forward units had to go on half rations because of difficulties in supplying them, he would place his head-quarters on half rations also.

He also insisted on no distinction between races or castes in the way troops were treated. The 14th Army included Indians, Africans and Gurkhas, as well as British soldiers, and Slim's ability to weld them into a cohesive whole provides an early example of the successful management of cultural diversity.

Dixon picks out three traits which are present in Slim's approach to the job of leading. First is his ability to work with people from different cultures, illustrated not only by his success in leading Gurkhas, Indians and Africans as well as Europeans, but also by his ability to build good relationships with the Chinese forces. The second characteristic was the absence of petty jealousy, exemplified in his relationship with the charismatic and celebrated Chindit leader, Orde Wingate, who attracted most of the media attention at the time.

Finally, Dixon points to the way in which Slim wholeheartedly cooperated with the Allied Air Forces, showing none of the inter-service rivalry which has characterized so many senior commanders.

A last lesson from Slim's case is about the dangers of stereotyping. When at Staff College he narrowly avoided failure because of his lack of aptitude for, or interest in, games.

# THATCHER'S LEADERSHIP LESSONS

What follows is an updated version of an article I wrote for *Director* magazine shortly after Margaret Thatcher's resignation. Time has not altered my views.

The leadership of Margaret Thatcher in the political arena offers several useful lessons for people in positions of power in industry and commerce. Clearly she was the kind of leader sometimes described as 'transformational', ie one who seeks and brings about radical change. Britain's industrial equivalents are managers such as Sir Colin Marshall and Sir John Harvey-Jones. Transformational leaders tend to share four characteristics. They possess a clear vision and strong sense of direction. Marshall, for example, wanted British Airways to be 'the world's favourite airline'; Harvey-Jones wanted ICI to be a '21st century chemical company, today'. Margaret Thatcher's vision was of a Britain restored to its former greatness.

Equally, values play an important role in providing the fuel for the transformational leader's energy. Strong beliefs help form the vision; they sustain the leader when his or her policies are under attack. Above all, they are the source of the leader's conviction that he or she knows best what the organization – or the country – needs.

Transformational leaders are also charismatic. They articulate the vision and give expression to their beliefs and values in ways that provoke both acceptance of their ideas and strong personal loyalties. This heady combination can, in some circumstances, lead to a dangerous mixture of adulation and sycophancy. Finally, they are capable of being quite ruthless in pursuit of what they think is right and are willing to take huge risks, often on the basis of a strong intuitive belief that things will work out in the end.

Thatcher, perhaps to a greater extent than any other leader in the post-war world, exemplifies the transformational power of leadership. Her strongly held system of values has passed into the language as Thatcherism. Her strong sense of direction – 'this lady's not for turning' – and her ruthless determination – 'the iron lady' – have become legendary. Her willingness to take huge risks was well illustrated by the gamble of the Falklands War. Her personal charisma created a degree of devotion both in her close colleagues in the government and in the Conservative party at large, which has probably not been equalled in British political life.

Studies of transformational leaders in industry attempt to identify the qualities possessed by such exceptional people. Thatcher appears to have most of them to a quite remarkable degree. A high energy level is one of the most important attributes: the ability to keep working very long hours, needing relatively little sleep and virtually always radiating energy to those around you. When the bomb exploded in the Grand Hotel, Brighton, just before 3 am, Margaret Thatcher was still working on her papers.

Another vital quality is the mental power which makes it possible to absorb, digest, retain and, when needed, recall, vast amounts of information about people, policies and programmes. Few leaders have rivalled Margaret Thatcher's extraordinary ability to keep closely in touch with details, while at the same time focusing on the major issues. As in the case of some highly regarded industrial leaders, this led to a reluctance to delegate and a tendency to interfere in the affairs of her lieutenants.

Courage is also essential and she displayed it frequently. Some aspects were clearly on view during the Falklands campaign and on the occasion of the Brighton bombing. Other, deeper aspects became apparent at the time of losing her support within the parliamentary party. Personal charm and charisma – less evident during television interviews than on other, more relaxed occasions – are, in her case, clearly of a very high order. It is a nice point that an anagram of her name is 'that great charmer'.

The list of positive attributes is long. One, however, is not just a vital ingredient of the mixture but constitutes the force that binds all the others together. That is the quite extraordinary level of self-belief, of conviction, of unshakeable certainty that one is right and that other viewpoints are misguided. This characterizes many transformational leaders and is perhaps Thatcher's outstanding quality.

This attribute can also be the transformational leader's Achilles' heel. Convinced of their own infallibility, they are their own worst enemies when it comes to challenges to their views. When they not only do not welcome such challenges, but in fact perceive them as disloyal, as Margaret Thatcher clearly did, then the weakness can prove irreparably damaging. This weakness is closely related to another aspect of her style of leadership – her failure to build a strong, cohesive and stable team. Building a set of strong personal loyalties with individuals is not the same as team-building. The government during the 1980s was never a team, not even during the Falklands crisis, and was in consequence less effective than it might have been. This, too, is a failing that can be seen in the behaviour of some of the nation's top business leaders.

Reluctance to accept the validity of opposing viewpoints carries with it another major potential danger. It weakens the leader's ability to make sound judgements about people when filling positions. Those who have 'sound opinions' – in other words, who agree with the boss – are preferred over those inclined to demonstrate independence of thought. Some of Thatcher's appointments can only be understood on this basis. The inadequacy of some of her ministers, quickly and cruelly exposed, served only to reinforce her own sense of being far and away more able than those around her. It was this lack of judgement of people, even of those whom she had every opportunity to study at close hand, which resulted in the first significant move against her – Sir Geoffrey Howe's resignation speech.

As with the transformational leaders of industry, however, the key question is whether she was an effective leader. If so, then with all its evident faults, the Thatcher style of leadership can serve as a role model. That leaves us with the question: how to produce more leaders in the same mould. If not, then there are equally important lessons to be learned, including how to prevent too much power ending up in the hands of one person.

There were two main things she set out to achieve – to increase Britain's standing and influence in the world and to reverse the process of economic decline at home. Both objectives involved a true conservatism in the sense that they represented a desire to restore former glories rather than discover alternative paths forward.

On the world stage there is no doubt that she gave a commanding performance. We British basked in the reflected glory of her personal triumphs in building the special relationships with Reagan and Gorbachev which made our nation, rather than Germany or France, the key European player in the drama that culminated in the ending of the Cold War. To carry the metaphor further, a graceful departure as the Berlin Wall was dismantled would have brought bouquets from all sides. As it was, her next appearance, playing opposite Bush rather than Reagan, and with the spotlight on European unity, drew boos and hisses from the front stalls as well as the gallery.

A similar judgement can be reached in respect of her domestic leadership, particularly in relation to the economy. Here her greatest achievement, and the one for which she will be remembered, was to arrest the very real decline in Britain's economic performance. Her attack was a three-pronged one. She set about returning the 'commanding heights' of the economy to private ownership; she deployed market forces to stimulate enterprise and risk-taking; and effectively she destroyed the militant and obstructive elements in the trade union movement.

By 1988, Britain's rate of economic growth matched or exceeded that of the other major trading nations; inflation was under control; the balance of payments was strong; employment was growing rapidly again. Although house prices were rising rapidly, interest rates were moderate and, with incomes rising fast, home-ownership was within the reach of young people on modest incomes. We had never had it so good – and again it was the time to bow out.

After 1988, slowly but surely, things started to go wrong again. The answer to the question of why things went so wrong lies in those very qualities which in the beginning contributed so much to Thatcher's success. A strong sense of direction is wonderful until the need to change direction occurs. When this happens, the leader who continues to stride determinedly along the same path, soon finds fewer and fewer followers trailing along behind.

A vision that is appropriate for one decade is unlikely to be valid or to have widespread appeal for the next. What the country needed, once its economy had been revitalised, was a fresh sense of direction – a vision not confined to the narrow, more materialistic objectives of gross domestic product, but a vision of the good society. Pollution, crime, inner-city decay, the 'cardboard cities', and the inadequate infrastructures for education, health and transport needed to be tackled with the same battling fervour with which inflation was tackled in the early 1980s. Both within the Conservative Party and in the nation at large the call for a more caring society was loud and clear. Yet it went largely unheeded. Indeed her major domestic policy error – the community charge – was seen as strong evidence of a different set of priorities.

In the international arena, the need was for a clear vision of Britain's role in Europe, one in which, through full partnership with other EC member states, Britain could play a leading role. Instead we were offered the prospect of becoming more and more isolated and increasingly less influential.

The lesson is clear. The task of the transformational leader is to transform. Once the job has been done, it is time to move on, to look for fresh challenges and new causes. Once Harvey-Jones had turned ICI round, he retired. Sir Ralph Halpern, having been Burton's saviour, stayed on too long. Tichy and Devanna (1986) question the capacity of any individual to lead an organization through multiple transformations. They point to such examples as Reginald Jones, who successfully led General Electric for a decade, and argue that of all his leadership acts, his most significant was the recognition that General Electric's future success demanded a leader with qualities and skills very different from his own. Margaret Thatcher's failure to see this in relation to Britain's future was perhaps her greatest weakness.

# JOHN HARVEY-JONES

John Harvey-Jones exemplifies the way in which childhood unhappiness, loneliness, a sense of inadequacy and of being unloved can drive a leader's will to succeed and to win the approval and recognition which have been lacking in early life.

He grew up in India until the age of six where his father was tutor to an Indian prince. Although he had a loving relationship with his mother, he felt ignored, rejected and humiliated by his father and in later life could not recall any warmth or affection in their relationship. Sent to preparatory school in England at the age of six, he did not see his mother again for three years. Not unnaturally, he felt utterly abandoned and uncared for. At school, he failed to make friends and was subject to bullying. He was to grow to believe that this period of his life developed in him the emotional resilience and self-reliance needed in top-level leadership. Relief came when, at the age of 13, he was accepted as a cadet by the Royal Navy. He enjoyed the disciplined life at the Royal Naval College, Dartmouth. During and after the Second World War he served in submarines and ended up at the end of the war commanding a German boat from which experience he learned about leading in a different cultural context.

At the age of 32, when his daughter was stricken with polio and he needed to be able to spend more time at home he left the Navy and joined ICI as a work study officer at Wilton. This job brought him into contact with people on the shopfloor and he learned to respect their skill and their capabilities. Moving through various roles in supply management and sales management he experienced, at the age of 40, something of a mid-life crisis affecting both his career and his personal, family life. He describes this with typical candour in his book *Getting it Together* (Harvey-Jones, 1992). Looking back, he feels that at that time he was putting too much energy into furthering his career as distinct from simply trying to do a good job. In 1967 he became a Divisional Director as Technical and Commercial Director, combining these duties with the unofficial role of assistant to the chairman; again a valuable learning experience, as was a subsequent spell as Personnel Director. At the age of 47 he became a very young (for ICI) chairman of Petrochemicals Division; a role he occupied for only three years before becoming a Main Board director. During this period he was thinking through his personal philosophy and approach to leadership, which he believed involved three fundamental requirements: having a vision; delegating; and projecting the organization's values. He also saw the need to maintain a healthy balance between business and family life.

In 1982 he became chairman of ICI which at the time was one of the two or three top jobs in British industry. Perhaps surprisingly in view of the success he achieved he described his time as chairman as the hardest and least enjoyable period of his life. He ascribed this to the political nature of the role, having to relate to different audiences, and to having to be 'on parade' all the time. He soon became prominent in the business world, not only because he successfully led ICI back into profit after the first loss in its history, but also because of his idiosyncratic appearance and his personality. He became well known for his long hair, large colourful ties and his high-pitched laugh; and well liked for the warmth of his personality and for his evident integrity.

In *Getting it Together* he dwells on the effects that power has on people and on his own efforts not to be seduced by it. He stresses the dangers that face top-level leaders when they begin to believe in their own infallibility.

In another book, *Making it Happen – Reflections on Leadership* (Harvey-Jones, 1989) he sets out his own philosophy and approach to the role. Right at the start he describes the basic beliefs which have guided him. For example, the belief that in pursuing an industrial career he was performing a social service since it is through the creation of wealth by its industry that a nation can afford to provide such things as a high quality of education and health care. He saw the principal function of management as 'maintaining the highest rate of change that the organization and the people within it can stand' and he acknowledged the need for the leader continually to adapt and learn. Openness features strongly in his system of values: '. . .those who will stand up without fear or favour and tell you, hopefully tactfully, that things are not really the way that everybody else thinks they are, are pearls beyond price.' Other values and beliefs which emerge from his writings include:

■ The importance of involvement and participation in decision making in generating commitment.

■ The need for goals to be stretching and challenging.

■ Tolerance of mistakes.

■ The importance of the individual.

Harvey-Jones' style was symbolized by his first act as chairman of ICI. He called a board meeting in his office instead of the boardroom. The board members were invited to sit round in a circle in comfortable conference chairs, each of which had an adjustable side table for papers. This became the accepted pattern There was no special order of seating and more often than not people sat in their shirt sleeves.

# ANDY LAW

Andy Law read Classics at Bristol University. After a spell in the City he began his career in advertising in 1978, joining the now defunct Wasey Campbell Ewald. In the 1980s he became the youngest ever Board Director of Collett, Dickinson Pearce International.

In January 1990 he helped establish a London office for the highly creative American agency Chiat/Day, becoming managing director in 1993. The turning point in his approach to leadership was his membership of a company task force set up by Jay Chiat in 1992 to 'study and construct what the Advertising Agency of the Future might look like'. The members of the task force christened themselves the Chrysalis Committee, the aim being to change the company as radically as a caterpillar changes and becomes a butterfly. 'The whole experience changed me and I realised that changing a company was a perpetual process, driven by a high ideal – like a long voyage of discovery, not a one-off plan that could be easily packaged and presented.'

A report with the title 'Something Else is Going On' was produced. It argued that business should be more ethical and play what was termed a Total Role in Society. The group took the view that if companies were to behave more like responsible citizens, they would avoid the embarrassment of running an expensive advertisement at the same time as receiving some adverse publicity due to some irresponsible act. As advertising professionals, they knew that this was a frequent occurrence; they called it 'Combined Inactivity', the paid-for publicity being cancelled out by the negative impact of the company's actions. The group debated the stakeholder concept and envisaged Chiat/Day as a company that would make money by doing good, working with companies to assess and review the way they were interacting with society. To the intense disappointment of its members the Chairman/Founder did not welcome the task force's report and the group was disbanded.

In 1994 Law was exposed to further stimulating ideas while working, on the Agency's behalf, with the Prince's Youth Trust. He saw business behaving in an enlightened philanthropic way, but wondered whether businesses could change the way they behaved so as to integrate more with society, rather than stand on the outside giving donations. He was taken with the concept of Human Capital and felt that it would be possible to unite the whole agency around this idea. He took the whole company of 30 people away for a weekend during which the aim would be to develop a better understanding of each other. They spent a full day doing things that challenged the boundaries of their comfort zones.

The next day Law decided to take the risk of being completely open about himself as a means of creating a high level of trust. He told about his early childhood in a home for 'Waifs and Strays' (literally). He revealed that his father was Indian, his mother English and that they had been teenage lovers whose relationship had been unacceptable both to the middle-class, church-going English community and the Sikh community of his father. Law was adopted at the age of three by a vicar and his wife and grew up in a series of vicarages in southern England. Law believes that from that day on he began to be seen as a managing director people could trust, in a company of people who would work hard to understand each other's strengths and weaknesses.

Another important influence was Anita Roddick and her exemplary company The Body Shop. After a number of meetings Chiat/Day was appointed The Body Shop's Agency for new media and internal communications.

In 1995 Jay Chiat sold his company to the US Corporation Omnicom. Law now led a management buy-out, having first checked that the London office's main clients –The Body Shop, Cable and Wireless, and The Midland Bank – would continue to support him and his team.

At this point Law took his team on another away day. The aim was 'to invent the perfect company'. The consensus to emerge was that everyone wanted an open, inclusive, creative company. The answer was found in a rare form of structure known as a Qualifying Employees Share Ownership Trust (QUEST). It was agreed that shares would be distributed equally to all employees, but that because Law had so much extra service and had made such a singular contribution he should have a 10 per cent stake, which he would only be able to realize in 10 years' time.

A year later Law changed this arrangement and gave up the 10 per cent deal. He had learned that 'unless you are prepared to give up something valuable you will never be able to truly change at all, because you'll be forever in control of the things you can't give up'. The fact that the senior executives of an agency held the same number of shares as the receptionist amazed people in the industry. For Law it was a major factor in the special nature of the company and its difference.

On the day St. Luke's was founded, 25 per cent of the trust's shares were distributed equally among the employees. Those who leave must sell their shares back to the trust. The government forgives any gain in share value as long as the proceeds are used to make a major capital investment such as a house or car. But employees need not leave to realize the value of their shares. They may sell part, but not all, of their shares at any time, thus guaranteeing that all employees are always stockholders.

Law gives several reasons for going down the path of shared ownership:

■ First, to have adopted the conventional model of a plc would have created an us-and-them, bosses and employees, divide that would have run counter to the aim of true cooperative working.

■ Secondly, it would have been theft of the work of the entire company whose spirited and imaginative serving of the clients caused clients to stay with the agency.

■ Thirdly, the few with shares would have been left at some future time having to have a sale strategy. But they wanted to create a company that would live beyond them, rather than create something and then destroy it for the sake of personal gain.

So it was decided that every employee would own shares after six months' qualifying service. This decision paid off in loyalty. Staff turnover has virtually disappeared and most departures were due to changes in people's personal circumstance rather than moving to another agency. Equally important has been the increase in client loyalty – a reflection of the improvement in the consistency of service delivered by a stable, committed workforce.

The name chosen for the new enterprise also caused some raised eyebrows. It was chosen because Saint Luke was the patron saint of creative people. To complete the picture of being different the agency eschewed London's smart West End offices and moved into a former toffee factory near Euston Station.

The organizational model adopted by the new company is based on three principles that are interconnected:

- Exploring. 'Our vision – "To Open Minds" – is there before us to remind us what will happen if we stop exploring. We will close down our potential imagination rather than open it up. That would lead to competitive disadvantage.'

- Meeting client deadlines with fascinating product.

- Being true to ourselves and our personal value systems. This is the responsibility of the six elected trustees of the Qualifying Employees Share Ownership Trust.

The problem of avoiding bureaucratic tendencies while growing has been tackled by what is termed the Citizen Cell Structure. This establishes highly autonomous groups of not more than 35 people. As these in turn grow, they must split, amoeba-like into smaller units.

Another Law initiative was to conduct a Social and Environmental Audit to establish a framework for ethical as well as financial and creative growth.

The success of this exciting venture is not in doubt. Having been runner up in 1996, St. Luke's was voted Agency of the Year by *Campaign* magazine in 1997. Among its successful and memorable campaigns have been one for IKEA ('Chuck out the chintz') and one for Eurostar, featuring the former Manchester United star Eric Cantona.

# 10

# The new leadership

The evolving nature of business conducted by global organizations will also call for a fundamentally different kind of leader. Gone are the days of top-down, hard-nosed direction. Demonstrating flexibility and empathy, while remaining true to the core values of the organization and finding ways to circumvent unpredictable impediments, will be characteristic of tomorrow's leaders. These will be people who are inspirational; technologically savvy but not prone to getting lost in details; entrepreneurial; devoted to service, and inclusive rather than independent or autocratic. Additional key leadership competencies will include: the ability to develop and articulate a value proposition – maintaining it in a dynamic market and energising others to buy into it; investing in a business model that guides employee decision-making at all levels, committing to a culture that values mentorship and learning while aligning individual and corporate goals, and recognising what it means to develop and manage truly transformational knowledge systems. The common characteristics of these new leaders are all related to issues that are more focused on the intangible aspects of an organization. Over time, those would-be leaders who are unwilling or unable to demonstrate these leadership behaviours will find themselves with few followers. (Nevins and Stumpf, 1999)

## THE END OF THE HERO?

The philosophy of leadership underlying the leadership development programmes of the past is no longer adequate for dealing with the complex problems inherent in communities and organizations today and in the future. This implicit philosophy assumes that leadership competence resides in individuals who are capable of inspiring and influencing others to solve problems and achieve goals. However, this 'heroic' view of leadership is often based on a deficient view of people, as Peter Senge (1996) points out. Especially in the West, leaders are heroes – great men (and occasionally women) who rise to the fore in times of crisis. This traditional view of leadership is based on assumptions of people's powerlessness, their lack of personal vision and their inability to master the forces of change, deficits that can be remedied only by a few great leaders.

Nicoll (1986) argues that the 'hero' or 'saviour' leader is largely mythical. The myth rests on our wish for leaders to be 'higher, stronger and better than we ourselves are: our saviours'. This desire, he points out, places huge burdens on the leaders. The myth also implies a passive followership role for the rest of us. It causes us to underestimate the importance of the interactive aspects of leader–follower relations. Nicoll suggests that direction and goals are 'not dreamed up and delivered to us by a leader'. These messages are 'created within and through our interaction with a leader'.

In Nicoll's view, leaders need to begin thinking about their responsibilities and roles 'in startlingly new ways' if they are to be effective in the emerging business environment. They need to see themselves as part of an 'action dialogue' or 'shared trusteeship'; as part of a mutual, interactive process. They need to remove some implicit prejudices from their thinking, for example the polarization of leader and follower roles, the hierarchic bias, the concept of the follower as passive.

Nicoll's views are echoed by Warren Bennis (1997), who argues that 'our contemporary views of leadership are entwined with notions of heroism, so much so that the distinction between "leader" and "hero" often becomes blurred. In our society leadership is too often seen as an inherently individual phenomenon.'

Collins and Porras (1994), in their major research project which looked at the factors associated with long-term sustained business success, concluded that 'a high profile, charismatic style is absolutely not required to successfully shape a visionary company'. They cite William McKnight, who served 3M successively as general manager (15 years), CEO (20 years) and chairman (17 years) – a soft-spoken, gentle man; humble, modest and unobtrusive. Others lacking obvious charismatic qualities include Bill Hewlett of Hewlett Packard, Bill Allen of Boeing, and George W. Merck.

## Level five leadership

Jim Collins (2001) led a research project in which the starting point was a search for companies that were truly transformed from being average performers into outstanding ones. He and his team began with 1,435 companies that appeared in the Fortune 500 list from 1965 to 1995. They looked for a particular pattern of stock market returns – 15 years at or below the average, then a transition point, followed by returns at least three times above the market average for the next 15 years. Only 11 companies matched the criteria. These averaged returns 6.9 times the market average for the 15 years after the transition point. This can be compared with the return of 2.8 times achieved by GE under Jack Welch between 1986 and 2000.

For each of the 11 companies the researchers picked a comparator based on similarity of business, size, age and performance in the period leading up to the transition. Six other companies were identified as 'unsustained' comparators – companies that showed only temporary improvement.

No less than 22 research associates worked on the project and they sifted through mountains of articles and company documents, conducted 87 interviews with executives and analysed masses of statistics. They then drew their conclusions, identifying the drivers of lasting transformation of performance.

Among these, what Collins calls 'level 5 leadership' was critical to success. Level 5 leaders are characterized by a seemingly paradoxical combination of humility and shyness on the one hand (Ying) and wilfulness and fearlessness on the other (Yang). Among the 'Ying' characteristics are shunning publicity, acting with quiet, calm determination, ambitious for the company rather than self, accepting full responsibility for failures, giving credit to others for success, developing successors. The 'Yang' qualities include unwavering resolve regardless of difficulties, and unwillingness to settle for anything but the best. (The idea of five levels of leadership was developed during the research and is built on the assumption that level 5 is a high level of leadership effectiveness that is founded on four other capabilities, starting with being a highly capable individual, then a contributing team member, then a competent manager and then an effective leader short of creating enduring greatness.)

Further evidence of a relationship between effective leadership and a degree of humility comes from a research project by The Industrial Society, now The Work Foundation, (1999). This involved asking some 3,000 observers to rate the performance of leaders on 38 competencies.

Each leader was asked to complete a self-rating and then four ratings were obtained anonymously from their immediate reports or from members of other teams in the same organization. The top 100 leaders in the sample were rated at 6.3 or above on a 7-point scale on all 38 items in the questionnaire. Their own self-ratings were, however, much more modest, scoring in most cases between 4.6 and 5.8. The bottom 100 leaders, by contrast, showed no such self-criticism, Their self rating scores showed that they had an inflated sense of their own abilities relative to the opinions of the observers.

Hooper and Potter (1997) point out that the key issue facing future leaders is 'Unlocking the enormous human potential by winning people's emotional support. . . our leaders of the future will have to be more competent, more articulate, more creative, more inspirational and more credible if they are going to win the hearts and minds of their followers.' In the following part of this chapter some relatively recent concepts of leadership that have a common focus on releasing human potential will be examined.

Kanter (1992) conjures up an image of a new kind of business hero who avoids the extremes of bureaucratic manager or 'corpocrat' on the one hand and 'maverick' on the other. Such a leader, she asserts, needs to cultivate the following skills and sensibilities:

▌ The ability to operate without the might of the hierarchy behind them.

▌ Knowing how to 'compete' so as to enhance cooperation – bearing in mind that competitors in one sphere may be collaborators in another.

▌ Operating with very high ethical standards.

▌ Having the kind of humility that accepts that there is always more to be learned.

▌ Being aware of the importance of process as distinct from substance or content.

▌ Deriving satisfaction from the achievement of results.

Rost and Smith (1992) offer a definition of the 'new' leadership as 'an influence relationship among leaders and followers who intend real changes that reflect the purposes mutually held by both leaders and followers'. They point out that influence is a process which can go in any direction, not just from the top down. Leaders and followers are actors in the influence process, although not all actors will exercise equal influence. Real changes are ones that are 'substantive and transforming' and which reflect what followers want as what leaders want. Rost and Smith suggest that people tend to give their support to others, ie to leaders or followers who meet certain criteria which they encapsulate as the '5 Cs of credibility'. They are:

▌ Character – honesty, trustworthiness and integrity.

▌ Care – concern for others' needs.

▌ Composure – the ability to cope gracefully with pressure.

▌ Courage – willingness to stand up for one's beliefs.

▌ Competence – both technical and interpersonal.

## WHITE WATER LEADERSHIP

White, Hodgson and Crainer (1996) stress the need for future leaders to be able to cope with uncertainty and turbulence:

> Leadership used to be about certainty. Throughout history, great leaders always appeared to know what to do. . . In the 1990s and beyond, instead of slow moving flows, leaders find themselves hurtling down rapids. White water leadership is the new corporate necessity. . . Now, the most strategically important aspects of an organization's future lie in the area of uncertainty. So, the first component which a leader has to learn to do differently is to learn to move towards uncertainty rather than away from it.

The five key skills essential to white water leadership are:

▌ **Difficult learning.** 'Learning is the key tool in this process, especially the ability to identify and learn the things that the individual or the organization find hard to learn.'

▌ **Maximizing energy.** 'A common feature of people who handle ambiguity well seems to be an easy access to energy, both in themselves and others.'

▌ **Resonant simplicity.** '. . .the leader who has the ability to capture the essence of an issue in a way that resonates with the rest of the organization is going to get the message through.'

- **Multiple focus.** For example, balancing the short term and the long term.

- **Mastering inner sense.** Following one's intuitive judgement in the absence of reliable data.

## THE LEADER AS COACH AND DEVELOPER

Bartlett and Ghoshal (1995) stress the need, in the future, for leaders to act more and more as coaches and developers. They cite Goran Lindahl, one of ABB's executive vice-presidents who sees acting as coach and developer as his most important role. Lindahl estimates that he spends 50–60 per cent of his time in this way.

Another example they give is Roger Enrico who, as vice-chairman of Pepsi-Co, committed half his own time to being on-call coach to Pepsi-Co's divisional presidents. He also set up a series of five-day retreats for managers of high potential, asking each invitee to bring with them 'a big idea', that is, a proposal that could have a big impact on the success of the business. Enrico conducted these sessions himself. At the end of each one, the attendees returned to their units to implement their projects and then, three months later, reconvened to report progress.

## LEADER/LEARNER

The things that are most difficult to learn are also the things that competitors will find difficult to learn; hence they are the sources of competitive advantage. Pfeffer (1994) argues that the supreme example of such a learning difficulty is how to create and sustain an internally consistent human resource strategy. Kay (1993) refers to the difficulty of learning how to create what he describes as the organization's 'architecture' – the network of relationships within and external to the organization.

Schein (1992) asserts that:

> The most intriguing leadership role in culture management is one in which the leader attempts to develop a learning organization. . . The learning leader must portray confidence that active problem solving leads to learning and, thereby, set an appropriate example for other members of the organization. . . The toughest problem here for learning leaders is to come to terms with their own lack of expertise and wisdom. . . The only

way to build a learning culture that continues to learn is for leaders themselves to realise that they do not know and must teach others to accept that they do not know. The learning task is then a shared responsibility.

Binney and Williams (1995) describe effective leaders as ones who both lead and learn – leading from a confident 'knowing' position and being willing at the same time to be open to challenge and new ideas. These leaders, they assert, have four characteristics:

▌ operational credibility, which is a function of having a deep understanding of the business, its products and the issues to do with it;

▌ being 'connected' to their organization – being in close touch with employees and customers;

▌ leading by example: if leaders practise 'Do as I say' rather than 'Do as I do', they will fail to be effective;

▌ consistency under pressure: for example, in being willing to com municate bad news as well as good news.

## Learning leadership in action: John Neill, CEO of Unipart

Unipart was created in 1987 by a management buyout of the parts division of the former state-owned British Leyland (now Rover, formerly a BMW subsidiary).

In an interview published in *Strategy*, the newsletter of the Strategic Planning Society, Neill (1997) tells how he turned round a company with a third rate manufacturing operation, struggling to meet quality and delivery requirements. 'We knew that if we were to succeed in manufacturing, we needed to learn from the best in the world.' The turning point came when the company won a contract with Honda because of the learning that Honda was willing to share with its new supplier. He sent a team of six people to study with Honda's fuel tank supplier in Japan and the result of this learning was a complete change in both management and production.

In 1993 Unipart U – the Company University – was established. It now offers 180 different courses that have been developed and are taught by Unipart staff. The courses are designed to be practical, so that attendees 'train for work' and can apply 'this morning's learning to this afternoon's job'. Within the 'University' is 'The Leading Edge', a state-of-the-art technology showroom and training centre where all employees can drop in at any time of the day to work out new ways in which technology can help them unlock their creative potential. There is also the 'Learning Curve', a learning resource centre that acts as a lending library for books and periodicals, provides access to online information, and even supplies laptop computers which employees can use at home.

## Creating a learning organization

The role of the learning leader in the learning organization has four aspects:

- A willingness not only to keep learning but also to be open about this, encouraging others to follow the leader's example and making it clear that there is no use sitting around and waiting for the leader to come up with the answers.

- The encouragement of learning by asking challenging, awkward questions, by stimulating intellectual curiosity.

- The ability to facilitate the learning of others, by acting as coach or mentor and by putting in place appropriate incentives, commissioning training and development programmes, and establishing facilities such as learning resource centres.

- The fostering of a culture that is supportive of learning. The principal characteristics of such a culture include: tolerance of mistakes and avoidance of blame; absence of 'not invented here' attitudes; a high level of cross-functional and interdisciplinary integration; encouragement of active membership of professional bodies; and strong emphasis on authority based on competence and expertise rather than rank or position power.

- The development of mechanisms for the transfer of learning from individuals and teams into the organization's store of knowledge and experience.

# STEWARDSHIP

Block (1993) argues the case for replacing our traditional concepts of leadership with a new concept: 'stewardship'. Most of our theories about making changes, he asserts, are clustered around the idea of leadership and the role of the leader in achieving the transformation of organizational performance. In his view, this pervasive and almost religious belief in leaders actually slows the process of genuine transformation. Stewardship is about 'the willingness to be accountable for some larger body than ourselves – an organization, a community'. It is to do with 'our choice for service over self-interest', with being 'willing to be deeply accountable without choosing to control the world around us'.

Block draws a basic distinction between 'good parenting' as an approach to the governance of organizations and 'partnership'. The former is based on the belief that those at the top are responsible for the success of the organization and the wellbeing of its members. Partnership is based on the principle of placing control close to where the work is done.

Another distinction is between dependency and empowerment. The former rests on the belief that the people in power know what is best and that it is their job to create a safe and predictable environment for the rest of us. Empowerment reflects the belief that the ability to get things right lies within each person and is our willingness to commit ourselves to making the organization work well, with or without the sponsorship of those above us.

The most fundamental distinction and choice, however, is between service and self-interest. Today our doubts about our leaders are not so much about their talents as about their integrity and trustworthiness. For Block, the 'antidote' to the seductive, but ultimately destructive, force of self-interest is to commit and adopt a cause – the cause of the place where we work.

He sees strong leadership as incapable of creating the fundamental changes which are needed in our organizations if they are to survive and prosper into the next century. 'It is not the fault of the people in these positions, it is the fault of the way we have framed the role.' The search for strong leadership reflects the desire we have that others should assume the ownership and responsibility for our organization. The result is to concentrate 'power, purpose and privilege' in the one we call leader.

In Block's view, we pay a price for our tendency to attribute to leaders the ability to transform organizations. He makes the subtle point that 'the leaders we are looking for have more effect in the news than in our lives'. The illusion of the great leader reinforces the idea that things are only achieved as a result of the actions of individuals so that we give credit to individuals for results that have in fact been produced by teams. We become over-dependent on sponsorship from the top as a means of winning support for our initiatives. The danger for the people at the top, of course, is that they begin to believe their own press cuttings.

Block's concept of partnership is a radical one. It poses four requirements.

■ The first of these is 'exchange of purpose'. Paternal leadership sees the organization's purpose and vision as set by the top, whereas partnership means 'each of us at every level is responsible for defining vision and values'. 'Purpose gets defined through dialogue.'

■ The second requirement is 'the right to say no'. Block concedes that, 'when all is said and done, others will have the right to tell us what to do'. But, he goes on, 'This has no effect on our right to say no. The notion that if you stand up you will get shot undermines partnership'.

■ Third, there is the requirement for 'joint accountability'. 'Bosses are no longer responsible for the morale, learning or career of their subordinates.' Accountability becomes widely distributed and linked to the rewards system.

■ Finally, there is the requirement for 'absolute honesty'.

Block's recipe does, however, fall short of anarchy. 'Partnership does not do away with hierarchy and we still need bosses.' Those at the higher levels, however, are responsible for 'clarity' rather than 'control'.

To act as 'steward' rather than 'leader' would involve operating on the following nine principles:

1. Maximize choice for those closest to the work.

2. Reintegrate the managing and the doing of the work. Everybody manages. Management becomes a set of tasks and activities, not a full-time job title. Everyone should do some of the core work of the organization. The higher the level in the organization, the more critical this becomes.

3. Measurements and controls should serve the core workers.

4. Support local solutions – do not press too hard for consistency across groups.

5. People are accountable to those they serve – their subordinates as well as their customers. Bosses are treated as suppliers, not as customers.

6. Staff groups (eg Human Resources) should have to sell their services and justify the value they add to teams of core workers.

7. End secrecy.

8. Exact an undertaking to commit to act in the best interests of the organization as a whole.

9. Redistribute wealth.

A business leader who exemplifies the stewardship concept is Dennis Bakke, co-founder of AES Corporation. AES is an international power company founded in 1981 that now has a turnover of over $3billion and operates over 140 power plants in some 46 countries. Bakke argues that 'the purpose of business and the purpose of AES is stewarding resources in order to meet a need in society'. Bakke believes that 'the stewardship of the earth and its resources for the benefit of all is a primary responsibility of mankind' (Manz and Sims, 2001).

# THE SERVANT LEADER

The term *servant leader* was first used by Greenleaf in 1970 in an essay entitled *The Servant as Leader* (1977), the first of a dozen essays or books on leadership which have sold more than half a million copies worldwide. Greenleaf spent the major part of his career with AT&T in the management education role, and went on to work as a consultant to several major institutions in the world of education. In 1964 he founded the Center for Applied Ethics, now known as the Robert K. Greenleaf Center.

Greenleaf was greatly influenced in his thinking by the novel *Journey to the East* by Hermane. This is an account of a journey undertaken by a group of people, members of a religious order, on some kind of spiritual quest. The central figure of the story is Leo, the party's servant, who accompanies the group and, through his sustaining influence, helps them to overcome difficulties. One day, however, Leo disappears. The group rapidly disintegrates and the quest is abandoned. The narrator decides to try and find Leo and, after many years' searching, finds him and discovers that he was, in fact, the head and guiding spirit of the Order, recognized as a wise and great leader. Greenleaf saw this parable as conveying the central idea of his own approach to leadership – that great leaders are those who serve others.

Spears, in his introduction to a book of essays in recognition of Greenleaf's work (1995) identifies the following 10 characteristics of the servant-leader from his study of Greenleaf's work:

1.  **Listening.** Servant-leaders make a deep commitment to listening intently to the vibes of others. They also listen to their own 'inner voice', seeking to understand the messages that their own bodies, minds and spirits are telling them. They spend time in reflection.

2.  **Empathy.** Striving to understand others; not rejecting them as people, while not accepting their behaviour or performance.

3.  **Healing.** In the sense of helping people to cope with emotional pain and suffering.

4.  **Awareness.** Sensitivity to what is going on, including self-awareness.

5.  **Persuasion.** Seeking to convince others of the rightness of a course of action rather than achieve compliance through coercion.

6.  **Conceptualization.** The ability to think in conceptual terms, to stretch the mind beyond day-to-day considerations.

7.  **Foresight.** The ability to understand the lessons from the past, the realities of the present and the likely future consequences of decisions.

8.  **Stewardship.** Seeing one's role in terms of holding in trust the wealth and resources of the organization for the benefit of society.

9.  **Commitment to the growth of people.** Valuing people beyond their contributions as employees and showing concern for their personal, professional and spiritual growth.

10. **Building community.** Creating a true sense of community among those who work in an organization.

Spears points to a number of ways in which the servant-leadership model has been influential in institutional life such as its adoption by leadership education programmes in both the profit and non-profit sectors.

One example of its adoption as a central philosophy by a business organization is TD Industries, a Dallas-based contracting company which has been profiled in Moskowitz's *The 100 Best Companies in America to Work For.* The company's founder, Jack Lowe, came across Greenleaf's ideas in the 1970s and began to distribute copies of his essay to his employees, who were invited to discuss it in groups. Since then all employees who supervise others first go through a training programme in servant-leadership and all new employees receive a copy of Greenleaf's essay.

Senge, writing in the same collection of essays states that *Servant Leadership* is 'the most singular and useful statement on leadership that I have read in the last 20 years'. Senge argues that the Western view of the management process is based on a particular model of how we move from a set of individual views to collective coordinated action. The model, which is tacit and assumed, involves a linear process. First a shared view of goals is established. While humanists argue for a participative process and the building of consensus, 'we all know that a more political model often dominates in real organizations.The boss's view prevails'.

The second step is to convert the shared goals into an action plan which includes role, reporting relationships and specific interim objectives. Finally there are control mechanisms to check how far the goals are being achieved and thereby leading to modifications of the plan. This model is proving to be inappropriate because the world is changing too fast for our plans to be implemented. Tight control from the centre no longer works like it used to. Organizations that cling too much to central controls, like IBM and General Motors, suffer 'a breakdown of the central nervous system'. The most common response to the breakdown of centralized management has been to decentralize decision making, empowering front line people to make decisions without referring upwards. But this fails to work because local people do not see or understand how their decisions affect other parts of the organization. Because of this, Senge asserts, most attempts at decentralization fail and result in recentralization.

He offers a different theory of coordinated action in which, instead of a linear process, people participate in 'a pool of common thought'. As people begin to think together they will begin to act together. Such ideas, while alien to traditional management thinkers, are well known to jazz musicians or members of top sports teams. Senge illustrates this concept in training executives by showing sequences from the film *Dances with Wolves*. There is a sequence of scenes in which the council of the North American Indian's tribe meets. There is a great deal of conflict, but members listen gravely to the views of others. There are frequent pauses for reflection. Typically there is no apparent convergence on major issues. The leader will say, 'These are complex issues. It is easy to become confused. We will have to talk some more'. When Western managers watch these scenes they have mixed feelings. They value the careful listening and the expressions of mutual respect but they point out that no decisions have been reached, no plans agreed. 'All they do is talk.'

In a later scene, however, we see the tribe engaged in a buffalo hunt. 'Rarely has a movie recorded such a moving mosaic of coordinated action. In a context where no simple action plan would suffice, where each actor must be acutely aware of one another, and where they ultimately must share responsibility for one another's safety, the tribe operates with a fluid grace that is stunning.'

Senge suggests that the tribe's ability to act together in this way is inseparable from their capacity for sitting together and talking. He sees the role of leadership in building the capacity of the tribe to work together to achieve their goals in a closely coordinated way as an example of servant-leadership in action.

Senge also draws a parallel between his own well known identification of systems thinking as the *Fifth Discipline* and Greenleaf's emphasis on conceptual thinking. 'I'm suggesting that the leadership's responsibility is to help people understand a complex world. Without such understanding, all the visions in the world may be of little value, and efforts to sustain effective action will be continually thwarted by actions that prevent enduring improvement.'

Senge illustrates the idea of systems thinking with the story of the man who on seeing a huge domino in his path, moves it, but fails to notice that there is a circle of dominoes and that by moving one he has set off a chain reaction of falling dominoes that will eventually crush him. He points out that in business life such chains of events may take a year or two to work themselves out, by which time, if the original executive is lucky he or she will have moved on and it is the successor who will be crushed.

# THE FIFTH DISCIPLINE

Although its title says nothing about leadership Senge's work, *The Fifth Discipline – The Art and Practice of the Learning Organisation* (1992) is in fact a very pertinent guide for the leaders of today and tomorrow. It is about leadership as the process of nurturing people's commitment to and capacity for learning at all levels of the organization.

The first of Senge's five disciplines is *Personal Mastery,* which involves a commitment to life-long learning and is about 'clarifying the things that really matter to us. . . living our lives in the service of our highest aspirations'. Next comes *Mental Models*. This discipline is about learning to become conscious of our own mental models and subjecting them to rigorous scrutiny so as to get closer to reality. The third discipline is *Building a Shared Vision*. Senge stresses the value of a genuine vision, as distinct from a vision statement. The leader's role is 'to unearth a picture of an attainable future' that is capable of fostering real commitment. To try and dictate a vision is usually counterproductive, but to offer one for consideration and debate can start a very powerful process.

*Team Learning* is discipline number four. It is vital since teams rather than individuals are the 'fundamental learning unit in modern organisations. . . unless teams learn the organisation cannot learn'. As we have seen, S*ystems Thinking* is the fifth discipline. It is essential if we are to see the interactions between things which make up the whole and if we are to be able to manage change effectively.

In the learning organization, the leader has three functions. He or she is *designer, steward* and *teacher*. The design work of leaders is about creating an organization's policies, strategies and systems and making them work. It is about integrating parts into a cohesive whole. The leader's first task lies in the field of vision, mission and values. The essence of leadership here is to design the learning processes. The leader's role as steward links directly with the ideas of Greenleaf and Block. Stewardship is to do with the long-term survival of the organization and with its contribution to the wider society. It provides an ethical foundation to the leader's role.

The leader as teacher is continually helping people to see 'the big picture': how the different parts of the organization interact, how apparently different situations have things in common, and the wider implications of today's decisions. Leaders who are designers, stewards and teachers see their core task as to bring about creative tension by highlighting the gap between reality and the vision: what John Harvey-Jones has called creating a deep sense of dissatisfaction with the *status quo*.

# THE LEADER AS EDUCATOR

Ronald A Heifetz is Director of the Leadership Education project at the John F Kennedy School of Government, Harvard University. In one of the most challenging books on leadership of recent times, Heifetz (1994) sets out the case for the leader as educator. In his view, real leaders 'influence the community to face its problems'. Rather than 'influence the community to adopt the leader's vision'. He offers five principles to guide leaders:

■ Identify the problem and the need for change; make clear to all the stakeholders the issues and values involved.

■ Recognize that change results in stress and that without stress it is unlikely that real change can take place. The leader's task is to contain the stress and keep it within tolerable limits.

■ Leaders should concentrate on the key issues and not be distracted by such things as personal attacks. They should not accept attempts to deny the problem exists.

■ They should give people responsibility at the rate they can stand and should put pressure on the people with the problem to contribute to its solution.

■ Protect those who contribute leadership even though they have no formal authority. People who raise tough questions and by so doing create stress should not be silenced – they can often provoke the rethinking of issues in ways which leaders with formal authority cannot.

These principles are extremely apposite in the case of those top-level business leaders, such as Bill Ford of the Ford Motor Company or Lord Browne of BP, who are wrestling with the problems of conflicting interests in the short term as they seek a path to a sustainable future for the stakeholders to whom they hold themselves accountable.

For Heifetz, strategy begins with asking which stakeholders have to adjust their ways in order to make progress in solving this problem? How can the leader strengthen the bonds that link the stakeholders, focusing on their community of interests, so that they can stand the stress of problem solving?

Facing up to conflict and to the realities of the situation are critical to leadership. Heifetz's ideas tie in with the concept of the learning organization and the need to expose underlying problems rather than treating immediate symptoms. Exercising leadership from a position of authority in change situations involves 'going against the grain' in that instead of meeting people's expectations that the leader will supply the answers, the leader asks pertinent questions.

Rather than shielding people from external threats the leader lets people feel the threat so as to stimulate a thirst for change. Rather than suppressing conflict the leader generates it; instead of maintaining and defending the *status quo*, the leader challenges it.

# SUMMARY

There is a growing consensus that the nature of the business environment as we move into the 21st century calls for a different type of business leader. Turbulence and uncertainty, coupled with changing attitudes to business on the part of society are creating a whole new set of expectations with regard to the characteristics of business leaders.

There is increasing disillusionment with the traditional view of the leader as a heroic figure, endowed with personal charisma. The number of 'fallen idols' in terms of reputations built and then lost has been steadily growing. In some cases the charismatic figure turns out to have been defrauding the company and its shareholders. Also, the importance of leader–follower relations is being increasingly recognized.

Among the qualities seen as desirable for 21st century leaders are:

- The ability to exercise influence without the backing of hierarchy or position power.

- High ethical standards.

- Humility and acceptance that one can always learn from others.

- Personal mastery.

- Valuing people and showing concern for their personal and professional development.

Role models that are alternatives to the charismatic hero have been suggested by a number of researchers, including:

- Leader as 'steward' – putting service before self-interest. 'Today our doubts about our leaders are not so much about their talents as about their integrity and trustworthiness' (Block, 1993).

- Servant leader: a similar concept. Stressing that leadership is about serving the community, not about exercising power and enjoying privilege.

- Level 5 leadership. Leaders who are characterized by a seemingly paradoxical combination of humility and shyness on the one hand (Ying) and wilfulness and fearlessness on the other (Yang).

■ Senge's five disciplines:

- Personal mastery – 'living our lives in service of our highest aspirations'.

- Mental models – awareness of our own way of looking at the world.

- Building a shared vision.

- Team learning – 'Unless teams learn, the organization cannot learn.'

- Systems thinking – insight into the relationship of the parts to the whole.

In Senge's view the leader has three roles:

■ Designer – creating policies, strategies and systems.

■ Steward.

■ Teacher.

Finally, Heifetz emphasizes the importance of the leader's role in meeting the expectations of all the organization's stakeholders, focusing on their community of interests and strengthening the bonds that link them.

# 11

# Summing up

## THE MAIN FINDINGS OF LEADERSHIP RESEARCH

### 1. Leadership defined

The word 'leadership' has several meanings. It can refer to a social *process*, a *personal quality*, a *role* in groups and organizations and, when used as *a collective noun*, to those responsible for the destiny of a country or a company.

### 2. Leadership as a social process

The leadership process involves actors who are both leaders and followers: it takes place in a given socio-technical context. Factors such as national or organizational culture or the nature of the task exercise a powerful influence on the way the process is carried on. From this it follows that the study of leadership cannot be validly carried on from a purely psychological perspective. It must be set within the context of the study of the decision-making processes and functioning of organizations.

### 3. Leadership and management

Leadership differs from management in important respects. The legitimacy of managerial authority comes from the holding of an office in which that authority has been invested. The legitimacy of leadership rests on the trust placed in the leader and on the leader's perceived competence and integrity. Management involves rational thought processes and the exercise of verbal and numerical intelligence. Leadership is more intuitive and involves emotional intelligence.

## 4. Leadership makes a difference

Leadership does make a difference to the performance of individuals, groups and organizations. It does so at the individual level by creating commitment as distinct from the compliance that is created by the exercise of formal authority. Committed people are inspired, enthusiastic, dedicated, energized and resolute. As such they are capable of greater accomplishments than those who are merely compliant and whose chief characteristic is apathy.

Leadership also improves the performance of groups and organizations by team-building, through its impact on group cohesion and by generating pride in collective achievements.

## 5. Leadership effectiveness exists at two levels

Effective leadership can be defined at two levels. The first level is when leadership is deemed to have been effective once the attitudes and/or behaviour of followers have been significantly influenced. The second level is when, as a consequence of that influence, the group is enabled to achieve goals that otherwise would not have been capable of achievement. In the Second World War Churchill was effective as a leader at the first level in that by his speeches and example he influenced people's attitudes so that they began to believe in the possibility of ultimate victory. He was also effective at the second, deeper level, in that his consistent leadership through the war years was instrumental in creating the resilience under attack on the part of the civilian population, which largely negated the German bombing offensive, and the high morale in the armed services that enabled them to put the early reverses behind them and regain the initiative.

## 6. Leadership is widely distributed

The study of leadership has been distorted by over-concentration on truly great world-class leaders. These cases are not necessarily the best to choose as role models, since people may despair of being able to emulate them. The thousands of 'working leaders' provide a better source of lessons for those who wish to improve leadership effectiveness, particularly when we are considering how to develop future leaders.

## 7. Leadership at different levels

There are important differences between different leadership levels in organizations. At lower levels the emphasis is on *interpersonal* leadership. At this level the leader's task is primarily to achieve short-term goals and to facilitate personal involvement and teamwork. The leadership that takes place in the higher echelons of large organizations involves *institutional* leadership. At this level leadership is about developing and maintaining systems of beliefs and values. The institutional leader deals with issues in terms of their long-range implications for the organization. His or her major functions are to define policy, to build the kind of social structure that will put that policy into effect, and to maintain the values and culture that will ensure its continuity.

## 8. Leadership is not just about change

Because the most well-known 'heroic' leaders in business and industry in recent years have been successful in bringing about organizational change the idea has grown up that the concepts of leadership and organizational transformation are inextricably linked. This is not so. Leadership is just as often also involved in maintaining traditional values in the face of challenges from those who wish to bring change about or in enabling groups of people to endure hardships.

## 9. Leadership traits

There is no one set of personality traits or qualities that are common to all effective leaders. Different situations call for different sets of personal qualities. Character – the expression in behaviour of a person's underlying values – is more relevant to effectiveness in a leadership role than intelligence, personality or other personal qualities.

## 10. Charismatic leadership

Some, but by no means all, effective leaders possess charisma. Charismatic leaders are people with a strong belief in the essential rightness of their own convictions. They are radical, unconventional, risk taking, visionary, entrepreneurial and exemplary. There is an intense emotional attachment to them on the part of their followers, which goes beyond such things as trust, respect or admiration to embrace awe, devotion and unswerving loyalty.

Other equally effective leaders, however, have low-key, quiet personalities – as much charisma as a dead mackerel.

## 11. The influence of early experience

A number of factors recur in biographical studies that cover the childhood and upbringing of outstanding leaders. One is *isolation* – either being separated from other children or the rest of the family or being bullied or unpopular. Another is unsatisfactory *relationships with parents*. A common pattern is an admired, demanding, domineering yet distant father. Another is that of a mother too busy with her career or social life to spend much time with her child. These patterns tend to produce two responses. One is self-reliance, not being dependent on the approval of others. Another is a strong drive to achieve, to prove oneself, to win, perhaps, the parental approval and applause that was lacking in the earlier years.

## 12. Leadership behaviour

The study of leadership behaviours is a more fruitful approach to a better understanding of leadership than attempts to list the qualities of effective leaders.

From the many studies of leader behaviour, the following emerge as closely related to effectiveness and in particular to the process of organizational transformation:

▌ developing a vision;

▌ articulating the vision and sharing it with followers;

▌ developing a set of shared values and beliefs;

▌ behaving consistently, being predictable;

▌ persistence in the face of obstacles or setbacks;

▌ communicating, telling stories, but also listening and learning;

- innovating;

- personal mastery, self-knowledge and self-discipline;

- visible leadership – walking the job;

- displaying self-confidence;

- demonstrating flexibility and coping with uncertainty;

- demonstrating calmness in crisis;

- delegating and empowering;

- acting as the group's representative and protector;

- matching rhetoric to action (do as I do, not do as I say),

- setting performance standards;

- learning and encouraging others to learn;

- providing recognition and reward.

## 13. Leadership styles

Research findings show that leadership styles vary in two main ways. First, there is a continuum of styles ranging from autocratic, through persuasive and consultative to participative. Secondly, leaders vary in the extent of concern they show for task accomplishment on the one hand and people's needs and expectations on the other. There is no single style likely to be effective in all circumstances. The effectiveness of a leadership style will vary according to the situation. This includes the general cultural setting in which leadership takes place and the extent to which the values of society are ones that favour autocratic or democratic forms of social control. Western societies are characterized generally by movement away from autocratically controlled social institutions and towards ones that are democratically constituted. This trend has inevitable implications for people's attitudes to the legitimacy of leadership and authority in the work situation. Increasingly, autocratic styles of leadership are being challenged not only in terms of their effectiveness but also on moral grounds. Leaders should be prepared to be flexible and adjust style to circumstances. At the same time they should avoid seeming to be inconsistent; if they adopt a different style in a particular set of circumstances the reasons for the change in style should be made clear to followers.

## 14. The situation is all-important

The effectiveness of leaders and of styles or patterns of leadership is contingent upon the situation, and in particular on the following:

▮ national culture;

▮ corporate or work group culture; for example, the pattern of effective leader behaviour would differ in a theatre company, a building site, a research laboratory and a soccer team;

▮ whether it is face-to-face leadership in a small work group or 'institutional' leadership of a complex organization;

▮ whether or not a widespread sense of crisis exists at the time;

▮ how experienced, well trained and competent the followers are.

## 15. Selecting future leaders

The selection of future leaders involves a number of intractable problems:

▮ First, there is the confusion between management and leadership to be resolved. Is the organization clear about what it wants? Managers, leaders or a combination of the two?

▮ Given that people who are currently in their twenties are unlikely in most instances to reach a senior position in a large organisation until their mid-thirties or later, there is a need to make a judgement about the future nature of organizations and business conditions and their implications for the nature of the leadership role. Given that there is reasonable confidence in such judgements, further judgements are needed in order to determine the qualities and skills that will be needed on the part of those who will fill such future roles.

▮ given that the qualities and skills that will be required have been reasonably well identified, there is the further need to identify which young people have the greatest potential for developing these qualities and attributes.

## 16. Approaches to the identification of potential

There are four main approaches to the identification of potential, which can be employed separately or in combination:

▌ Appraisal of potential by superiors, peers and/or subordinates. (When all three are employed the term 360-degree appraisal is used.)

▌ Psychometric tests of intelligence and personality factors.

▌ Questionnaire inventories that focus on leadership competencies.

▌ Assessment centres that involve individual and group tasks as well as a range of tests and interviews.

Evidence concerning the validity of these various approaches is mixed in quality and variable in its results. Long-term validation of selection methods in the business sector is very rare.

## 17. Pitfalls in identifying 'high flyers'

Given the very real difficulties associated with the process of validly identifying high flyers, it is not surprising that there are serious doubts about the whole process. Two potential pitfalls are commonly stressed. The first is the natural tendency for senior managers, when assessing leadership potential and selecting 'high flyers', to choose people in their own image and people who seem to fit in well, thus perpetuating the existing organizational culture rather than preparing it for radical change. The second pitfall is the self-fulfilling prophecy. If the young managers who are initially chosen to be part of the accelerated development programme for high flyers are then given early responsibility and other development opportunities, they will more or less automatically rise up through the hierarchy, provided they don't make any disastrous errors, while their erstwhile colleagues, deprived of such opportunities, never get the chance to show what, given similar privileged opportunities for development, they might have achieved.

## 18. Leaders are made rather than born

Leadership skills cannot be taught 'but they can be learnt or, rather, discovered, fostered and allowed to grow' (Handy, 1992).

## 19. Training courses and development programmes

It is important to distinguish between leadership development programmes and leadership training courses. A course, as the term implies, is a single event that may last anything from a day to several weeks, the purpose of which is to improve the effectiveness in leadership of those attending. A leadership development programme, however, is a series of related events including courses but also such things as mentoring and coaching, job assignments, attendance at an assessment/development centre, learning sets and/or various forms of feedback.

## 20.  Access to development programmes

In the majority of cases, where leadership development programmes exist, involvement in them is confined to so-called 'high flyers' – young men and women, usually graduates, who are identified as having the potential to attain senior management positions in a hierarchical structure. In only a minority of cases is this kind of development opportunity open to others such as knowledge professionals or technicians, let alone front-line employees in production or customer service.

## 21.  The importance of job assignments

A key element in any leadership development programme is the opportunities for learning offered by job assignments. The early assumption of real responsibility is seen as providing particularly useful experience from which many lessons may be learnt, subject to appropriate feedback and coaching.

## 22.  Other developmental policies and practices

Other practices that can aid the development of leadership competence include:

▌ assessment/development centres;

▌ career planning discussions with bosses;

▌ rewarding managers for developing their subordinates;

▌ helping people develop the capacity to manage their own development;

▌ mentoring and/or coaching;

▌ the use of feedback;

▌ adding additional responsibilities to current jobs;

▌ opportunities at a later career stage to broaden out through such experiences as a lateral move to a different function, attendance on a lengthy general management course, secondment to a voluntary organization or assignment to a special project team;

▌ a decentralized organization structure that pushes responsibility down to lower levels; Johnson and Johnson, 3M, Hewlett Packard and General Electric are quoted by Kotter (1988) as prime examples, while in Europe ABB has a similar structure;

▌ Processes that ensure that young employees are visible to senior management.

## 23. Shortcomings of leadership training

Leadership training programmes have some serious flaws. Many of them are more about management skills than they are about leadership, focusing on things like objective setting or management by objectives. Also, employers make the mistake of believing that training programmes will, by themselves, develop leaders. Leadership development must start at the point of recruitment. Job experiences, rewards and organization cultures must be combined with training to foster leadership potential and encourage the acquisition of the requisite skills.

## 24. Cultural differences

Leadership theories current in the management literature have largely originated in the United States. These theories are not necessarily valid in other societies with differing values and traditions. To use the same leadership processes without regard to national context is to risk at least mild misunderstanding and private amusement. At worst, it risks a fundamental but unrecognized clash of values that can only create problems for the smooth functioning of organizations. International teams differ from single-nationality teams because of the additional complexities that stem from such factors as different languages and communication styles, different ways of looking at the world and processing information, different behavioural expectations, and different stereotypes held by team members of each other. These additional complexities demand much greater attention to the team process.

## 25. Leadership in an international context

The key skills required for leadership in an international context include:

▌ how to work with cultures different from one's own;

▌ how to run a business that is international in scope;

▌ how to lead and manage people unlike oneself;

▌ how to handle a complex array of often difficult relationships;

▌ how to develop the skills and attitudes necessary for effective personal behaviour;

▌ how to know oneself to preserve and enhance one's family relationships and to manage one's own career.

## 26. Gender issues

The assumption that the leader is in control and knows the answers is frequently construed as a particularly masculine notion. The popular literature suggests the existence of a distinctive feminine style of leadership, characterized by greater willingness to listen, being more empathetic and people oriented and less aggressive in the pursuit of goals compared with males. Not all research findings bear this out. Some studies, however, have found differences. In these, women were seen to use a more democratic, participative approach, compared with a more autocratic, directive style used by men.

# References

Adair, J (1984) *The Skills of Leadership*, Gower, Aldershot

Adams, J D and Spencer, S (1986) The strategic leadership perspective, in *Transforming Leadership,* ed J Adams, Miles River Press, Alexandria, VA, pp 5–12

Andersen Consulting Institute for Strategic Change (1999) *The Evolving Role of Executive Leadership*, Andersen Consulting, London

Ashridge Management College (1988) *Management for the Future,* Ashridge Management College, Berkhamsted

Aspen Institute (2001) *No More Grey Pinstripes*, Aspen Institute, Aspen, CO

Badaracco, J L Jr and Ellsworth, R R (1989) *Leadership and the Quest for Integrity*, Harvard Business School Press, Boston, MA

Bartlett, C A and Ghoshal, S (1995) Changing the role of top management. Beyond systems to people, *Harvard Business Review,* May–June, pp 132–42

Bass, B M (1992) Assessing the charismatic leader, in *Frontiers of Leadership*, ed M Syrett and C Hogg, Blackwell, Oxford, pp 414–18

Bass, B M and Avolio, B J (1990) Developing transformational leadership – 1992 and beyond, *Journal of European Industrial Training*, **14**, pp 21–27

Bavelas, A (1969) Leadership: man and function, in *Leadership*, ed C A Gibb, Penguin (Modern Psychology Series), Harmondsworth

Behling, O and McFillen, J M (1996) A syncretical model of charismatic transformational leadership, *Group and Organizational Management*, **21** (2), pp 163–85

Bennis, W (1997) *Organizing Genius*, Addison Wesley, Reading, MA

Bennis, W (1999) The leadership advantage, *Leader to Leader*, **12**, Spring

Bennis, W and Nanus, B (1985) *Leadership: Strategies for taking charge*, Harper and Row, New York

Binney, C and Williams, C (1995) *Leaning into the Future*, Nicholas Brealey, London

Blake, R and Mouton, S (1964) *The Managerial Grid*, Gulf Publishing, Houston, TX

Blinkhorn, S and Johnson, C (1991) Personality tests: the great debate, *Personnel Management*, pp 38–42

Block, P (1993) *Stewardship*, Berrett Koehler, San Francisco, CA

Bruce, J (1986) *The Intuitive Pragmatists*, Center for Creative Leadership, Greensboro, NC

Clark, K E and Clark, M B (1994) *Choosing to Lead*, Leadership Press, Greensboro, NC

Collins, J (1996) Aligning action and values, *Leader to Leader*, Summer

Collins, J (2001) Level 5 leadership, *Harvard Business Review*, **79** (1), pp 67–76

Collins J and Porras, J (1994) *Built to Last,* Century, London

Cox, C J and Cooper, C (1988) *High Flyers*, Basil Blackwell, Oxford

Crabb, S (1992) *Personnel Management*, February, p 13

Crainer, S (1996) (ed) *Leaders on Leadership*, Institute of Management Foundation, Corby

Cunningham, I (1986) Leadership development – mapping the field (unpublished paper), Ashridge Management College, Berkhamsted

Davison, S C and Ward, K (1999) *Leading International Teams,* McGraw-Hill, New York

Deering, A, Dilts, R and Russell, J (2002) *Alpha Leadership: Tools for business leaders who want more from life*, Wiley, New York

Dixon, N (1976) *On the Psychology of Military Incompetence*, Jonathan Cape, London

Drucker P (1969) *The Age of Discontinuity*, Heinemann, London

Drucker, P (1992) Leadership – more doing than dash, in *Managing for the Future*, Butterworth-Heinemann, Oxford, pp 100–03

Durcan, J (1994) *Leadership: A question of culture*, Ashridge, Berkhamsted

Evans, P (1992) Developing leaders and managing development, *European Management Journal*, **10** (1), pp 1–9

Farkas, C M and Wetlaufer, S (1996) The ways chief executive officers lead, *Harvard Business Review*, May–June, pp 110–22

Fiedler, F (1969) Leadership – a new model, in *Leadership*, ed C A Gibb, Penguin, Harmondsworth

Fleishman, E A (1973) Twenty years of consideration and structure, in *Current Developments in the Study of Leadership*, eds E A Fleishman and J G Hunt Southern Illinois University Press, Carbondale, IL, pp 2–3

Gardner, H (1996) *Leading Minds*, HarperCollins, London

Grant, J (1992) Women as managers. What they can offer organisations, in *Frontiers of Leadership*, ed M Syrett and C Hogg, Blackwell, Oxford, pp 298–306

Greenleaf, R (1977) *Servant Leadership*, Paulist Press, New York

Guest, R (1962) *Organisational Change. The effects of successful leadership*, Tavistock, London

Hampden-Turner, C and Trompenaars, F (1993) *The Seven Cultures of Capitalism*, Doubleday, New York

Handy, C (1992) The language of leadership, in *Frontiers of Leadership*, ed M Syrett and C Hogg, Blackwell, Oxford, pp 7–12

Harvey-Jones, J (1989) *Making it Happen*, Fontana, London

Harvey-Jones, J (1992) *Getting it Together*, Mandarin Paperbacks, London

Heifetz, R A (1994) *Leadership Without Easy Answers*, Harvard University Press, Boston, MA

Hersey, P and Blanchard, K (1988) *Management of Organizational Behaviour: Utilizing human resources*, Prentice-Hall, Englewood Cliffs, NJ

Hind, P (1999) Leaderabilities, *Directions*, April, Ashridge, Berkhamsted, pp 20–26

Hirsh, S K and Kummerow, J M (1987) *Introduction to Type in Organizations*, Consulting Psychologists Press Inc, New York

Hodgson, P and White, R P (2001) Effective Leader, *Directions*, Ashridge, Berkhamsted, Summer, pp 18–22

Hofstede, G (1991) *Cultures and Organisations*, McGraw-Hill, Maidenhead

Hooijberg, R and DiTomaso, N (1996) Leadership in and of demographically diverse organizations, *Leadership Quarterly*, **7** (1), pp 1–19

Hooper, A and Potter, J (1997) *The Business of Leadership*, Ashgate, Aldershot

The Industrial Society (1999) *Liberating Leadership*, The Industrial Society (now The Work Foundation), London

Kahn, R L (1956) The prediction of productivity, *Journal of Social Issues*, **12**, pp 41–49

Kanter, R M (1992) In search of the post-industrial hero, in *Frontiers of Leadership*, ed M Syrett and C Hogg, Blackwell, Oxford

Kanter, R M (1999) The enduring skills of change leaders, *Leader to Leader*, **13**, Summer, pp 73–78

Katz, D (1950) *Productivity, Supervision and Morale in an Office Situation*, Institute for Social Research, Ann Arbour, MI

Kay, J (1993) *The Foundations of Corporate Success*, Oxford University Press, Oxford

Kets de Vries, M (1994) The mystique of leadership, *Academy of Management Executive*, **8** (3), pp 29–45

Kotter, J P (1988) *The Leadership Factor*, Free Press, New York

Kotter, J P (1990) What leaders really do, *Harvard Business Review,* May–June

Kotter, J P (1998) Winning at change, *Leader to Leader*, **10**, Fall

Likert, R (1961) *New Patterns of Management*, McGraw-Hill, New York

Lock, D (1988) *Handbook of Management*, 2nd edn, Gower, Aldershot

Lombardo, M M (1988) *The Dynamics of Executive Derailment*, Technical Report, **34**, Center for Creative Leadership, Greensboro, NC

Maccoby, M (2000) Narcissistic leaders, *Harvard Business Review*, Jan, pp 69–78

Manz, C C and Sims, H Jr (2001) *The New SuperLeadership*, Berrett-Koehler, San Francisco

McCall, M W Jr (1998) *High Flyers: Developing the next generation of leaders,* Harvard Business School Press, Boston, MA

McCall, M W Jr and Hollenbeck, G P (2002) *Developing Global Executives*, Harvard Business School Press, Boston, MA

McCall, M W Jr, Lombardo, M M and Morrison, A M (1988) *The Lessons of Experience*, Lexington Books, Lexington, MA

McCauley, C (1986) *Developmental Experiences in Managerial Work. A Literature Review*, Technical Report, **26**, Center for Creative Leadership, Greensboro, NC

McGregor Burns, J (1978) *Leadership*, Harper and Row, New York

Mintzberg, H (1999) Managing Quietly, *Leader to Leader*, **12**, Spring

Morrison, A M, White, R P and Van Velsor, E (1987) *Breaking the Glass Ceiling*, Addison Wesley, Reading, MA

National Council for Education in Management and Leadership (2001) *Leadership Development: Best practice for organizations,* National Council for Education in Management and Leadership, London

Neill, J (1997) interview in *Strategy*, Journal of the Strategic Planning Society, London, April

Nevins, M and Stumpf, S (1999) 21st century leadership, *Journal of Strategy and Business*, 3rd quarter, pp 1–15

Nicoll, David (1986) Leadership and followership, in *Transforming Leadership*, ed J D Adams, Miles River Press, Alexandria, VA

Norburn, D (1989) The Chief Executive – a breed apart?, *Strategic Management Journal*, **10**, pp 59–64

Ochse, R (1990) *Before the Gates of Excellence*, Cambridge University Press, Cambridge

Pascale, R (1990) *Managing on the Edge*, Penguin Books, Harmondsworth

Peters, T (1987) *Thriving on Chaos*, Macmillan, Basingstoke

Peters, T (1992) *Liberation Management*, Macmillan, Basingstoke

Pfeffer, J (1994) *Competitive Advantage Through People*, Harvard Business School Press, Boston, MA

Reddin, W J (1970) *Managerial Effectiveness*, McGraw-Hill, Maidenhead

Roberts, W (1992) In the Roman Court: leadership qualities, in *Frontiers of Leadership*, ed M Syrett and C Hogg, Blackwell, Oxford

Roddick, A (2000) Leader as social advocate: building business by building community, *Leader to Leader*, **17**, Summer, pp 87–113

Rosener, J B (1990) Ways women lead, *Harvard Business Review*, November, pp 119–25

Rost, J and Smith, A (1992) Leadership: a post-industrial approach, *European Management Journal*, **10** (2), June

Sadler, P (1966) *Leadership Style, Confidence in Management and Job Satisfaction*, Ashridge, Berkhamsted

Sadler, P (1988) *Managerial Leadership*, Gower, Aldershot

Sadler P (1993) *Managing Talent*, FT/Pitman, London

Sadler, P and Hofstede, G (1976) Leadership styles: preferences and perceptions of employees of an international company in different countries, *International Studies of Management and Organization*, **6** (3)

Sayles, L R (1993) *The Working Leader*, The Free Press, New York

Schein, E (1992) *Organizational Culture and Leadership*, Jossey-Bass, San Francisco

Selznick, P (1957) *Leadership in Administration*, Row Peterson, Evanston, IL

Semler, R (1993) *Maverick*, Century, London

Senge, P (1992) *The Fifth Discipline*, Century Business, London

Senge, P (1996) The ecology of leadership, *Leader to Leader*, **2**, Fall, pp 39–51

Slim, Field Marshal Lord (1956) *Defeat into Victory*, Cassell, London

Smith, P B (1992) Organizational behaviour and national cultures, *British Journal of Management*, **3**, pp 90–97

Spears, L (1995) Servant leadership and the Greenleaf legacy, in *Reflections on Leadership*, ed L Spears, John Wiley and Sons, New York

Storr, A (1969) The man, in *Churchill, Four Faces and the Man*, The Dial Press, New York, pp 203–46

Syrett, M and Hogg, C (eds) (1992) Leadership – the attitudes and opinions of European leaders, *Frontiers of Leadership*, Blackwell, Oxford

Tannenbaum, R and Schmidt, W H (1958) How to choose a leadership pattern, *Harvard Business Review*, **36**, pp 95–101

Tichy, N M and Devanna, M A (1986) *The Transformational Leader*, Wiley, New York

Trompenaars, F and Hampden-Turner, C (2001) *21 Leaders for the 21st Century*, Capstone, Oxford

Van Seters, D A and Field, R H G (1990) The evolution of leadership theory, *Journal of Organizational Change Management*, **3** (3)

Welch, J (2001) *Jack, Straight from the Gut*, Headline, London

Westley, F and Mintzberg, H (1989) Visionary leadership and strategic management, *Strategic Management Journal*, **10**, pp 17–32

White, R and Lippit, R (1959) Leader behaviour and member reaction in three social climates, in G*roup Dynamics, Research and Theory*, ed D Cartwright and A Zander, Tavistock, London

White, R P, Hodgson, P and Crainer, S (1996) *The Future of Leadership, a White Water Revolution*, Pitman Publishing, London

Wills, S (1996) European leadership: key issues, *European Management Journal*, **14** (1), February

Zaleznik, A (1992a) Managers and leaders: are they different?, *Harvard Business Review*, March–April, pp 126–135

Zaleznik, A (1992b) How leaders develop, *Harvard Business Review*, March–April

# Index

# THE *MBA MASTERCLASS* SERIES

The new *MBA Masterclass* series is designed to meet the needs of both MBA students and experienced managers looking for a refresher course in a particular subject.

Authoritative but practical, these titles focus on MBA core subjects as well as covering the latest developments in management thinking and practice.

Written by international academics, consultants and practitioners, this series is an ideal companion for any busy MBA student or manager.

Current titles published in the series:

> *Leadership*
> *Intercultural Management*
> *Strategic Management*

And still to be published:

> *Project Management*
> *Branding*
> *Finance and Accounting*
> *Human Resource Management*

To obtain further information, please contact the publisher at the address below:

Kogan Page Limited
120 Pentonville Road
London N1 9JN
Tel: +44 (0) 20 7278 0433
Fax: +44 (0) 20 7837 6348
www.kogan-page.co.uk